Wildy Practice Guides

Residential Tenancies

Richard Colbey

and

Niamh O'Brien

Wildy, Simmonds and Hill Publishing 2009

© 2009 Wildy, Simmonds & Hill Publishing

The right of Richard Colbey and Niamh O'Brien to be identified as the authors of this Work has been asserted by them in accordance with sections 77 and 78 of the Copyright, Designs and Patents Act 1988

First published in Great Britain 2009 by Wildy, Simmonds & Hill Publishing

Website: www.wildy.com

Colbey, Richard

Residential Tenancies (Wildy Practice Guides series)

1

2 C

I Title II O'Brien, Niamh

ISBN 9780854900428

Printed and bound in Great Britain

Preface

After a break of nearly a decade I am delighted that Wildy has offered to take on the task of producing this book. I do so hope that the book, which has lasted longer in the field than its two previous publishers, Longmans and Cavendish, does not exert its possible jinx, over what has been one of the gentlest and most accommodating businesses I have ever worked with. While remaining in a positive mode I am equally delighted that my colleague in Lamb Chambers Niamh O'Brien has agreed to undertake the task of updating the law, and has done so with great insight and diligence.

Niamh's task has been made no simpler by the fact that there have been little in the way of seismic shifts in the area so far this millennium. Much of the changes have been procedural, and perhaps not always for the good. The plethora of prescribed forms make things more difficult for landlords, tenants, their lawyers and even many judges, than allowing the parties to identify and set out what they considered were the important aspects of the case in Particulars of Claim and Defences. One of the more important, and I hope successful, objects of this book is to enable readers to get these forms right and avoid the delay and wasted costs that result all too often from the most minor and excusable failure to comply.

The most significant new substantive area of law may be in respect of the deposit protection schemes. These are surely to be welcomed. So many landlords abused the power they had over the deposit, conjuring up non-existent defects or simply ignoring the tenants' request for its return altogether. How great the practical impact of the scheme will be is another matter. Anything that is dependent upon an application to the court is immediately outside the range of what is likely to be done by a majority of tenants. Nonetheless, by in a small way drawing this law to the legal profession's attention I hope we are contributing to a culture where this minor but worthy piece of law reform benefits tenants.

The main theme of the prefaces to the two previous works has been the loss of security of tenure since the Housing Act 1996 came into force. Of course, virtually no new tenancies with meaningful of security are now being granted, and my observations are no different than they were 15 years ago. Niamh's research, which appears in the introductory chapter, shows that there are likely to be well over 100,000 tenancies subject to the much greater protection of the Rent Act 1977 still in existence. Each one of those represents a long-term –

over 20 years – home provided at a reasonable rent. The 1977 Act and its predecessors were some of the most radical wealth redistributing legislation the country has ever seen. Of course, whether or not that is a good thing is a matter on which there is no consensus, and while I make little attempt to hide my views, I hope that has never clouded what should be an objective commentary on the law. The opportunities for profits to be made by 'buy to let landlords' were not there when this legislation prevailed up until 1989, but the social impact was tremendous. It is significant that even the 'reforming' Conservative government of the 1980s waited nearly 10 years before significantly watering down such protection, in the Housing Act 1988, and another 8 years before abolishing it altogether. The issue of reverting to security of tenure now seems to be off the 'political agenda'. Certainly, there has been no hint that new Labour, which may identify more with buy to let landlords than their tenants, has any such plans, and the Law Commission's proposals seem to have attracted little governmental support.

On a lighter note, I cannot say I have devoted the time to this edition as I have to previous ones, so the expressions of gratitude to my family, swelled by the addition of Ned in 2004, need to be so effusive. There have been few recordable incidents of any Monsters, as they are generally known in the parenting trade, attempting to hijack my computer away from 'boring writing'. The advent of wireless broadband and the retention of an old computer in the hall has made the life of an author/parent so much easier. Nonetheless, they do like to see their names in print, and so to the more obviously deserving of gratitude Niamh O'Brien and Andrew of Wildy, I add thanks to Sarah, James, Melanie and Ned as well as my lovely (and indeed only) wife Emma.

Richard Colbey

Contents

1 Basic Information

1.1 Introduction

The book aims to be a concise guide to the law and practice of residential tenancies. The constraint of space has necessitated careful selection of the material so that discussion of some tenancies which could be regarded as falling within this field has been omitted. In particular, those seeking enlightenment on public sector tenancies, long leases and agricultural residential tenancies, to name the most significant omissions, will have to look elsewhere. The statutory law which forms the backbone of the subject matter of this book was substantially overhauled by the Housing Act (HA) 1988, which applies to all private sector residential tenancies granted on or after 15 January 1989. This in turn was amended by the HA 1996, which applies where the tenancy was granted on or after 28 February 1997. Neither Act has retrospective effect. Therefore, the earlier legislation, largely contained in the Rent Act (RA) 1977, still remains important, as most tenancies granted before 1989 are still governed by it and are dealt with separately in Chapter 4. It may seem an unnecessary inclusion, given that any tenancies governed by the RA 1977 were granted at least 20 years ago. However, because these tenancies are valuable assets to many tenants, in a way later tenancies are not, they do lead to more closely fought litigation, and while perhaps not numerically significant they still provide a substantial amount of work for lawyers working in the field. According to research published by the Department for Communities and Local Government as at 2007 there were 139,000 Rent Act tenancies still in existence, amounting to 6% of the total.[1] In this book both sets of statutory codes are dealt with separately, though with greater emphasis on the later legislation. Recent proposals by the Law Commission to substantially overhaul and simplify the law relating to landlord and tenant appear to have stalled and there are as yet there are no plans to introduce the Commission's draft Bill to Parliament. It seems highly likely therefore that this book will, we hope, be useful for many years in dealing with problems arising out of both pre-HA 1988 and post-HA 1988 tenancies.

1 See Department for Communities and Local Government, live tables on rents, lettings and tenancies, Table 731 www.communities.gov.uk.

1.2   Sources

1.2.1   Statute

Residential landlord and tenant law derives mainly from statute. The principal legislation is contained in the HA 1988. This Act had the effect of repealing the RA 1977 in respect of all but a tiny handful of new tenancies. It laid down a scheme of security of tenure and (very limited) rent control. It was a reflection of the then government's wish to eradicate legal control of the private sector housing market. A stated aim behind its introduction was to encourage more investment in the private sector, thus making more housing available. The aim has probably succeeded in as much as there is a greater degree of reasonable quality rented housing available for young working people, most of whom do not see themselves as having a long-term future in the rented sector. The private sector, however, is increasingly becoming an irrelevance to those at the bottom end of the market. While the growth of housing association tenancies, which are generally covered by the same legislation as the true private sector, has gone some way to counter the eradication of local authority housing, most people on low incomes or benefits do not even think of properties owned by private landlords as an option any more.

The RA 1977, the last in a long series of Rent Acts, sets out the tenant's right to security of tenure and the fair rent provisions. That Act was significantly amended by the HA 1980 and, to a lesser extent, by the HA 1985. It still applies to all qualifying tenancies granted before 15 January 1989.

The Protection from Eviction Act 1977 gives tenants and other residential occupiers protection from being evicted other than through the courts. The security afforded by the Protection from Eviction Act 1977 is often the only protection against summary eviction afforded to those tenants who lack security of tenure. In particular, the Act makes it a criminal offence to evict occupiers protected under the Act without a court order. However, not all occupiers of residential accommodation have even this limited protection.

The HA 1988 introduced the concept of the assured and the assured shorthold tenancy. In many respects the security of tenure offered by an assured tenancy was not vastly different to that afforded under the RA 1977. However, the assured shorthold tenancy had very limited security. It was envisaged that landlords could choose to grant shorthold tenancies as long as certain procedural conditions were met. However, as many landlords were unaware of what those conditions were, they sometimes unintentionally granted assured tenancies with full security of tenure. In this book all references to assured tenancies include assured shorthold tenancies unless the same are specifically excluded.

The main effect of the HA 1996 was to make all new tenancies, by default, assured shorthold tenancies, which means that a landlord need only wait 6 months from the commencement of a tenancy to regain possession if he so wishes. A landlord may still grant an assured tenancy with full security of tenure. Most assured non-shorthold tenancies granted after the coming in to force of the HA 1996 tend to be granted by housing associations and other public sector landlords.

The HA 2004 was primarily concerned with public sector tenancies but it also significantly altered the law relating to deposits payable by assured shorthold tenants at the commencement of their tenancy. These provisions apply to all tenancies granted after 6 April 2007. The Act also introduced a scheme of mandatory licensing for houses in multiple occupation.

1.2.2 Secondary legislation

The relevant secondary legislation deals mainly with forms. There are a number of notices which relate to the grant or termination of tenancies that have to be served in a prescribed form. These are contained in statutory instruments. All statutory instruments which have come into force since 1987 can now be found online at the website of the Office of Public Sector Information (www.opsi.gov.uk).

1.2.3 Procedural rules

Part 55 of the Civil Procedure Rules sets out the procedure for the commencement and management of possession proceedings relating to land. It is supplemented by a Practice Direction. Both Part 55 and the Practice Direction are set out at Appendix B. The Civil Procedure Rules and their accompanying Practice Directions and Pre-action Protocols can be viewed online at www.justice.gov.uk.

1.2.4 Common law

There are some areas which are not touched on by statute or statutory instrument at all. Notable amongst these is the vexed question of whether a particular agreement is a tenancy or a licence. Additionally, common law principles can become important when, for whatever reason, an occupier of residential accommodation does not have, or has lost, the protection of the statutes outlined below.

1.3   Outline of the Statutory Provisions

1.3.1   Tenancies granted before 15 January 1989

The RA 1977 (to which most residential tenancies granted prior to 15 January 1989 are subject) provides an elaborate scheme for the assessment of fair rents and security of tenure for residential tenants. The legislation generally applies where the occupier is a tenant rather than a licencee. In *Street v Mountford* [1985] AC 809, the House of Lords reiterated that the principal test for determining whether or not a residential occupier is a tenant is whether or not he has exclusive possession: if he does, he can qualify as a tenant. That test has, to some extent, been qualified by subsequent decisions and, as explained below; exclusive possession will not suffice in every case (see para 2.3.1). During a residential tenant's contractual term, he is known as a protected tenant. At the end of that contractual term, he will become a statutory tenant. Certain tenancies are excluded from being protected or statutory (see para 4.3). Protected and statutory tenants have, except in prescribed circumstances, security of tenure, which overrides any contractual right to possession the landlord may have. The landlord must go to court to recover possession and may only do so on certain prescribed grounds, usually relating to the tenant's misconduct or breach of tenancy agreement.

Even if the court finds that the grounds upon which possession is sought are made out the court will usually only grant a possession order if it is reasonable to do so

Most of the provisions that give the court discretion as to whether or not to order possession are contained in Part 1 of Sch 15 to the RA 1977. The provisions that give the landlord an automatic right to possession are contained in Part 2 of Sch 15 to the RA 1977. A landlord will have an automatic right to possession where the premises have been used, or were intended, for one of a number of specified purposes before the tenancy commenced and the tenant was told of this in writing before the tenancy commenced and the property is now required for that purpose.

A landlord who wished to be sure of obtaining possession could grant a protected shorthold tenancy. This had to be for a term between 1 and 5 years, and the tenant had to be given a notice in the prescribed form before its commencement. Once the term expired, Case 19 of Sch 15 gave the landlord a right to recover possession so long as he followed the correct procedure. That right continued, even if the tenant were allowed to remain in occupation after the expiry of the agreed term.

Part IV of the 1977 Act provides for a system of registration of 'fair rent'. Either a residential tenant or landlord may apply to the Rent Service (formally to the Rent Officer) to assess a figure for the maximum rent payable for the premises. This figure historically has tended to be well below the market rent. The right to make this application to the rent service cannot be excluded by an agreement between the landlord and the tenant. In the event that either party is not satisfied with the Rent Service's assessment he or she can appeal to the Rent Assessment Committee.

An important qualification of the scheme of security of tenure and rent control exists where there is a tenancy, but it is excluded from protection because the landlord is resident in the same building as the tenant, or where board is provided to the tenant. In those circumstances then there will be a restricted contract rather than a tenancy. Certain licences where the licencee has the right to occupy exclusively part of the premises were also restricted contracts. There is a limited amount of security of tenure and rent control available to such licencees. However the effluxion of time since the passing of the HA 1988 has rendered these provisions all but obsolete.

1.3.2 Tenancies granted on or after 15 January 1989

The HA 1988 provided a rather more rudimentary scheme for giving tenants security of tenure and a limited right to have a rent determined independently of the agreement between the landlord and the tenant. These parts of the Act apply only to tenancies and do not apply to licences. During a tenant's contractual term, he is an assured tenant. At the expiry of that term, if he is still in occupation, he automatically becomes a statutory periodic tenant under a continuing statutory periodic tenancy. Certain tenancies are excluded from being assured or periodic statutory tenancies and are listed in Sch 1 to the HA 1988 (see para 3.3). Excluded entirely from security of tenure and rent assessment provisions of the HA 1988 are tenancies where the landlord has resided and continues to reside in the same building as the tenant. Assured tenants can be evicted only on certain grounds, some discretionary and some mandatory, which are listed in Sch II to the HA 1988. Some grounds relate to the tenant's misconduct, including mandatory grounds where the tenant has been particularly recalcitrant in paying rent. Some grounds are dependent on a notice having been served before the commencement of the tenancy.

Under the 1988 Act, a tenant is not entitled to have any independent assessment of the rent when the tenancy is granted. Once the landlord wishes to raise the rent, he must first serve the tenant with notice of his intentions. The tenant has the right to refer the contract to a Rent

Assessment Committee, which will prevent the landlord raising the rent above the ordinary market rent of that property. The tenant cannot refer the rent payable during the fixed term (if any) to the rent assessment committee. He or she may only refer the rent payable in respect of a periodic tenancy or statutory periodic tenancy (where the agreed term has expired).

1.3.3   Tenancies granted on or after 28 February 1997

The HA 1996 reduced still further the protection of tenants. Section 96 of that Act provides that, from 28th February 1997, all new tenancies will be assured shorthold unless the parties expressly agree otherwise. However, in certain restricted circumstances a new tenancy may be a fully assured non-shorthold tenancy even if granted after that date. The most important exceptions to the HA 1996 are new tenancies granted where the parties are the same as under a pre-existing assured tenancy and the tenant has not served a notice on the tenant stating that the new tenancy is to be shorthold. In other words, the new tenancy will only be shorthold if the tenant wishes it (see further 3.7.2). Tenancies subject to the RA 1977 still retain their protection even if renewed after February 1997.

1.4   Glossary

Assured shorthold

Either: (a) a tenancy first granted between tenancy 15 January 1989 and 28 February 1997 inclusive that would otherwise have been an assured tenancy but for the parties' agreement that it is to be shorthold; or (b) a tenancy granted after 28 February 1997 which the parties have not expressly agreed will be fully assured.

Assured tenancy

A residential tenancy granted on or after 15 January 1989, which is not excluded by statute from being such a tenancy. In practice 'assured tenancy' may be used to refer solely to non-shorthold assured tenancies with full security of tenure. However, in this book any reference to 'assured tenancies' includes assured shorthold tenancies unless specifically excluded.

Break clause

A provision in a tenancy that enables either the landlord or the tenant to terminate it before the term expires.

Common parts

Parts of a property retained by the landlord and not let to any tenant. Examples are communal hallways, roofs, basements, etc.

Company let

The letting of residential premises to a company is usually described this way. Companies cannot be assured tenants under the HA 1988 or statutory tenants under the RA 1977. Residential tenancies granted to companies are governed by the terms of the agreement and the common law rules relating to landlord and tenant.

Covenant

A term of a tenancy. Can be either express or in limited circumstances implied, or implied specifically by statute.

Demise

The act of granting a lease or tenancy of a property. Also refers to the extent of the property that has been let under the lease/ tenancy.

Dwelling house

The unit of property that can become the subject of a protected tenancy, statutory tenancy, assured tenancy or periodic statutory tenancy. In effect, it means a self contained home. It can certainly include units such as flats and 'bedsits' which are not normally regarded as houses.

Excluded tenancy/licence

A tenancy/licence which is not protected by any of the statutory codes and does not have the benefit of the Protection from Eviction Act 1977.

Fair rent

The rent assessed by the rent service when an application is made to register a rent in respect of an RA 1977 tenancy.

Forfeiture

A right reserved to the landlord to re-enter the property if the tenant is in breach of a covenant of a tenancy agreement. A right of re-entry can arise only out of an express covenant contained in the tenancy agreement. There are substantial statutory restraints put on a landlord's power to exercise his right to forfeit and it is not generally used as a method for recovering possession of residential property.

Joint tenancy

A tenancy held by two or more tenants.

Lease

An agreement under which someone agrees to let another have exclusive possession of a property. Colloquially, though not in strict legal theory, tends to be reserved as a description for longer agreements. A lease amounts to a proprietary interest in the land, albeit of limited duration.

Licence

A personal permission to occupy land, whether in exchange for payment or not. This does not give the licencee the rights of a tenant and does not amount to an interest in the land.

Mesne profits

A sum payable by a trespasser in a property in lieu of a rent. Where a court has made an order evicting a tenant, but allows him to remain in occupation for a period, he will no longer be a tenant, but technically a trespasser, and hence liable to pay *mesne* (pronounced mean) profits rather than rent. Sometimes referred to as 'damages for use and occupation' where the 'trespasser' is a former tenant.

Notice to quit

A notice given by a landlord or tenant purporting to terminate a contractual periodic tenancy. In the case of a periodic tenancy or licence of a dwelling house, the landlord must give the tenant at least 28 days' notice of termination notwithstanding anything in the tenancy agreement allowing shorter notice to be given (s 5 of the Protection from Eviction Act 1977). In respect of assured tenancies, this notice has been replaced by the notice provided for in s 8 of the HA 1988.

Notice seeking possession

Notice served by the landlord on an assured tenant informing him of his intention to go to court to recover possession and the grounds upon which he intends to rely.

Periodic statutory tenancy

The tenancy that will arise after the expiry of the contractual term of an assured tenancy (s 5 of the HA 1988), sometimes called an 'assured periodic tenancy'.

Periodic tenancy

A tenancy with no fixed termination date which is renewed automatically at the beginning of each new period, eg week to week, month to month, etc. It will continue to exist until it is brought to an end by an appropriate notice.

Protected shorthold

A tenancy granted before 15 January 1989 that would otherwise have been a protected tenancy, but which is granted for a fixed term of between 1 and 5 years in respect of which a notice telling the tenant it is to be a shorthold tenancy has been served (s 52 of the HA 1980).

Protected tenancy

An RA 1977 tenancy of a dwelling house during its contractual term (s 1 of the RA 1977).

Registered rent

The fair rent assessed by the rent service in respect of a protected or statutory tenancy.

Regulated tenancies

The generic term for protected and statutory tenancies (s 18 of the RA 1977).

Rent Assessment Committee

The panel, usually consisting of three members, which hears appeals from assessments of fair rent by the Rent Service (s 65 of the RA 1977) and applications for determination of a proposed rent increase in respect of assured tenancies under the HA 1988. Part of the Residential Property Tribunal Service.

Rent Service

The body given statutory authority over various matters concerning rent: most importantly, the assessment of fair rents (Part IV of the RA 1977), formally referred to as the Rent Officer. Part of the Department of Work and Pensions.

Restricted contract

An agreement entered into before the commencement date of the HA 1988 under which a person is allowed exclusively to occupy a dwelling house, but which is not a protected tenancy because the lessor is resident or because the lessee is provided with board (s 19 of the RA 1977). Now obsolete.

Secure tenancy

A tenancy that would otherwise be a protected or assured tenancy, but which is granted by a specified public or charitable body. Most council houses are let on secure tenancies (s 79 of the HA 1985).

Service tenancy

> A tenancy granted to an employee for the better performance of his employment. Such tenancies usually have no or limited statutory protection.

Shorthold tenancy

> See assured shorthold tenancy and protected shorthold tenancy.

Statutory tenancy

> The tenancy that will arise once the contractual RA 1977 protected tenancy has come to an end. Can, though rarely is, also be used to describe the periodic tenancy which arises when an assured tenancy finishes.

Surrender

> The voluntary giving up of possession of rented premises by a tenant.

Term

> The period of time for which it is agreed that the tenancy will subsist.

Term of years

> Another name for a lease or tenancy.

2 The Nature of the Agreement

2.1 Introduction

When considering an occupant of residential premises it is important to correctly identify the legal basis upon which his right to occupy exists. This may not be obvious. It may be that he occupies pursuant to a tenancy, even if the parties have never discussed precisely the legal basis upon which the occupier would reside in the property in question. However, it may be that the nature of the agreement and the circumstances that surround it preclude the creation of a tenancy. It may be that the accommodation itself cannot, as a matter of law, be the subject of a tenancy. In such circumstances the occupancy must be referable to some other kind of legal arrangement such as a contract or a licence. As the protection afforded by the law to a residential occupier will differ according to his legal status it is vital establish what that status is.

2.2 Form of the agreement

It is not necessary to have a signed written agreement in order for a tenancy to exist.. It is possible for a tenancy to be granted orally. Further, a court may imply the grant of a tenancy where the actions of the parties (eg permitting someone to exclusively occupy premises in return for payment) are consistent with the grant of a tenancy. This may be so even if the parties never agreed or even discussed the legal basis under which one would occupy land belonging to the other. There is no legal requirement for a tenancy agreement to be in writing as long as the agreed term does not exceed 3 years (s 2(5)(a) of the Law Reform (Miscellaneous Provisions) Act 1989). If there is no express agreement as to the term of the tenancy it will be a periodic tenancy which will continue indefinitely until one of the parties takes steps to bring it to an end.

2.3 Tenancies and licences

Both tenancies and licences can be described as agreements for the occupation of land. However, a tenancy amounts to an interest in the land itself, albeit one of limited duration. The tenant has a legal right to exclude the world at large from the land, his landlord included. A licence is no more than a personal right of occupation. The question of whether or not an agreement for the occupation of accommodation amounts to a tenancy or to a licence is one that is very important in determining the relationship between the parties to that agreement. The distinction is particularly important in the residential sphere, as it determines whether or not the Housing Act (HA) 1988 (or as the case may be the Rent Act (RA) 1977) applies. It is not a distinction touched on at all by statute. The issue is more likely to arise in litigation relating to RA tenancies, as the relative ease with which landlords can recover possession under the HA 1988 reduces the incentive to attempt to avoid the creation of a tenancy. The leading authority is *Street v Mountford* [1985] AC 809, HL. Mr Street had granted Mrs Mountford the right to occupy a furnished room under a written agreement which purported to be a 'personal licence'. Mrs Mountford had exclusive possession of the room. She applied to have a fair rent assessed in respect of the room. The Rent Officer had jurisdiction only if she were a tenant. The House of Lords eventually came to decide the issue. They decided in favour of a tenancy. Probably the most important points that can be extracted from Lord Templeman's speech, which was the only substantive one given, were that:

(a)   where exclusive possession of premises is granted to a person in return for payment there will, unless there are special circumstances which suggest the contrary, be a tenancy;

(b)   the wording of any agreement the parties made was not crucial in determining whether or not exclusive possession had in fact been granted; and

(c)   the courts should disregard the existence of the Rent Acts in deciding whether or not exclusive possession had been granted.

This decision makes it clear that property owners will not be able to avoid creating a tenancy by giving occupiers an agreement which purports to be a licence, but which is, in reality, a tenancy because exclusive possession has been granted. If the occupier is excluded from the premises for part of the day, he is unlikely to be a tenant (*Asian v Murphy* [1989] 39 EG 109, CA). A mere gesture by the landlord towards retaining a right of occupation for himself, such as keeping a key, will not be sufficient to prevent there being exclusive possession (*Family Housing Association v Jones* [1990] 1 WLR 779, CA). In *Street v Mountford*, Lord Templeman contrasted the tenant with a lodger, who does not have exclusive possession of any part of the premises, although he may exclusively occupy, for instance, one room. A lodger is someone, according to his Lordship (*Street v Mountford*, p 818A), for whom:

... the landlord provides attendance or services which require the landlord or his servants to exercise unrestrained access to and use of the premises. The whole of the agreement should be construed to decide whether or not the occupier was merely a lodger. Once it was established that he was not a lodger, if he were paying a regular sum in respect of his occupancy, whether or not described as "rent", he would normally be a tenant. The position would be different only if there were special circumstances indicating that it had not been intended by the parties that he would occupy as a tenant.

Lord Templeman gave as examples an occupancy under a contract to sell land or pursuant to an employment contract or where the parties had no intention to create legal relations at all. The Court of Appeal found that there were such exceptional circumstances in *Sharp v MacArthur* [1987] 19 HLR 364. There, the defendant had been let into possession of a house which was vacant and available for sale, having told the plaintiff that he was in dire need of accommodation. Although he paid a rent and was given a rent book, this was held not to amount to a tenancy. This decision may be of some comfort to property owners considering granting short-term 'licences' from altruistic motives. Nonetheless, it does not set such a clear precedent that one can safely advise that there will be no tenancy in the circumstances.

2.3.1   Recent developments

In recent years the courts have been even less inclined to imply the creation of a tenancy where the circumstances of the case indicate that this was not the true intention of the parties, notwithstanding the fact that the occupier may have exclusive possession and pay for his or her occupation. For example in the case of *Vesely v Levy* (2007) NPC 52 the Court of Appeal held that an occupier who had exclusive possession of part of a flat and who had agreed to pay a weekly sum to the owner was not a tenant because the primary purpose of her entering into occupation of the property was to act as unofficial carer for a third party who resided in another part of the flat. Similarly in *Mansfield District Council v Langridge* (2007) EWCH 3152 (QB) the court held that an occupier who had been granted exclusive possession of a dwelling and who paid 'rent' was not a tenant. The purpose of the grant in that case was to house the occupier temporarily pending the resolution of legal proceedings relating to another property. It may be that these are merely examples of Lord Templeman's 'special circumstances', or it may demonstrate a greater willingness by the courts to permit the intentions of the parties to prevail where it is clear that they did not intend to create a tenancy, notwithstanding the grant of exclusive possession in return for payment.

2.3.2   Exclusive possession

Authoritative though *Street v Mountford* is on the lease/licence distinction, it does not assist where there is an argument about whether or not exclusive possession has actually been granted. The Court of Appeal has held that it is wrong for a judge simply to ask himself whether a residential occupier is a tenant or a lodger without first considering the question of exclusive possession (*Brooker Settled Estates v Ayres* [1987] 1 EGLR 500). This leaves open the possibility that property owners may be able to avoid the HA 1988 by using agreements entered into independently with more than one occupier, allowing each occupier to live in the property in common with the other occupiers, but having exclusive possession of no part of it. Such an agreement had been held to amount to only a licence in *Somma v Hazelhurst* [1978] 1 WLR 1014, CA, a case which was expressly overruled in *Street v Mountford*. However, the overruling of *Somma v Hazelhurst* may be explained on the basis that the agreement there was clearly a sham. The occupiers there had been a cohabiting couple who, in reality, would not have been asked to share their room with anyone else even if one of them had left.

'Sharing agreements' were considered by the House of Lords in *AG Securities v Vaughan; Antoniades v Villiers* [1990] AC 417. The House overturned the decisions of the Court of Appeal in both of these cases. In *Antoniades v Villiers*, the agreement was considered to be a sham, as the occupiers were living together as husband and wife and it was inconceivable that the landlord would have required them to share with anyone else. However, in *AG Securities v Vaughan*, each of the four occupants entered into their respective agreements on different dates, for different periods and were paying different 'rents'. This agreement was genuine and the House held there could not be a joint tenancy granted to the four occupiers. These cases suggest that it will be much harder to grant a 'sharing agreement' (as opposed to a tenancy) on a group of occupiers who approach the landlord together. Making the occupiers jointly and severally liable for each other's rent is likely to be fatal to any attempt to avoid a tenancy (cf *Mikeover Ltd v Brady* [1989] 3 All ER 618). In practice, it will often be difficult to draw up an agreement which avoids the grant of a tenancy. Certainly, the courts will not attach a great deal of weight to clever drafting which attempts to hide the reality of any agreement. If a property owner does request his legal advisers to attempt this, there can be no objection to trying to draft, for instance, a 'sharing agreement'. The owner, however, must be informed that there is no guarantee that such drafting will succeed. Even if it does, the owner may well face costly proceedings to establish that there is no tenancy. Given the ease with which most landlords can regain possession of property let on an assured shorthold tenancy there seems little point in doing so.

2.4 Exceptions

2.4.1 Employees

Employees who reside in accommodation owned by their employers may not have the benefit of a tenancy even though they pay rent and have exclusive possession. A common example would be a caretaker residing on or near school property. Where it is an express term of the contract of employment that the employee live in or near his or her place of employment, he or she will be a licensee and not a tenant. Such licensees are frequently referred to as 'service occupiers' and they have little security of tenure. It must be a genuine requirement of the contract of employment that the employee live 'on site'. In other words, it must genuinely assist the employee in the performance of his or her duties. Where the contract is silent on the point but it is nevertheless necessary (as opposed to desirable) that the employee reside on or near the place of employment in order to carry out his or her duties then the employee will be a licensee and not a tenant. If the employee is a service occupier his or her licence will usually determine on the termination of the contract of employment. However, landlords who wish to recover possession of premises occupied by a former employee will frequently serve a Notice to Quit before bringing possession proceedings without prejudice to any right that they may have to recover possession following the determination of the contract of employment.

If the employee is a tenant rather than a licensee then the landlord/ former employer can bring an action for possession based on Ground 16 to Sch 2 to the HA 1988. This discretionary ground for possession will only be available where the dwelling house was let to the former employee 'in consequence of his employment'. There is a similar discretionary ground for possession contained within the RA 1977 (Sch 15, Case 6). However, in those cases to which the RA 1977 applies the landlord must additionally establish that he or she requires the property back so that it can be let to another employee.

2.4.2 Resident landlords

Occupiers who share accommodation with the landlord or a member of his family are not usually tenants but lodgers or licensees. There is no reason in law why a residential occupier cannot grant a tenancy of part of his dwelling however the courts are slow to infer the existence of a tenancy in such circumstances even if the 'tenant' was in practice the only person who used that part (see *Monmouth BC v Marlog* (1994) 27 HLR 30). Even if there is a tenancy it cannot be an assured or assured shorthold as it is excluded by para 1 of Sch 1 to the HA 1988. Further both tenancies and licences where the occupier shares accommodation with the landlord or a member of the landlord's family are excluded from the operation of the Protection from Eviction Act 1977 (s 3A). An occupier will not be precluded from being a tenant merely because he or she occupies a dwelling which had previously been occupied by the landlord as his home. However, where a landlord occupied the premises prior to the commencement of a tenancy this may in certain circumstances afford him an additional ground for possession against both HA 1988 tenants (see para 3.3) and RA 1977 tenants (see para 4.3).

2.4.3   Agreements not relating to land

Only land can be the subject matter of a tenancy. Land is defined in s 205 of the Law of Property Act 1925 as including:

'Land of any tenure and mines and minerals whether not held apart from the surface, buildings or parts of buildings (whether the division is horizontal vertical or made in any other way) …'

It has been held that a permanently moored houseboat was not the subject of tenancy (*Chelsea Yacht and Boat Co Ltd v Pope* [2000] 1 WLR 1941, CA). The Act only applies to lettings of land and, although the boat was classified as a dwelling, it was not annexed to the land to an extent that made it part of the land.

Similarly, lettings of mobile homes will not normally be subject to the RA 1977 or the HA 1988, though a bungalow which could only be removed from land by being demolished will be, even in the absence of direct attachment between the land and the bungalow (*Elitestone v Morris* [1997] 1 WLR 687, HL).

The occupiers of mobile homes and caravans are usually licencees of the ground upon which the dwelling is positioned. In many cases the mobile home has been purchased by the occupier from the owner of the site under a hire purchase agreement. The rights of such occupiers are contained in the Mobile Homes Act 1983 and the Caravan Sites Act 1968 and not the general law of landlord and tenant.

3 Assured Tenancies

3.1 Introduction

The vast majority of private sector tenancies in existence are by now assured tenancies. A substantial majority of those will be assured shorthold tenancies. When considering the legal status any occupier of residential premises it is important to determine whether his occupation fulfils the requirements for an assured tenancy, as there is no such thing as an assured licence. It is possible for an occupier to fulfil all of the requirements of a tenancy (and not fall into any of the exceptions set out in Chapter 2) but nevertheless not qualify for assured status. In those circumstances his rights will be regulated by the tenancy agreement and the general law of landlord and tenant.

3.2 Requirements

In order to qualify as an assured or assured shorthold, a tenancy must fulfil the following requirements:

- The tenant(s) must be an individual (as opposed to a company or other corporate body).

- The demised premises must be a separate dwelling, ie a single self contained unit of accommodation.

- The tenants or at least one of them must occupy the dwelling as his only or principal home.

3.2.1 Tenant as individual

The grant of an assured tenancy under the Housing Act (HA) 1988 is conditional upon the tenant being a private individual. A company cannot be an assured tenant. In the past landlords sometimes required prospective tenants to form companies so that the premises could be let to them without attracting the protection of the Rent Act (RA) 1977. Landlords are now far less likely to resort to this device as most new tenancies have very limited security of tenure.

3.2.2 Separate dwelling

Section 1 of the HA 1988 refers to 'a dwelling house let as a separate dwelling'. However, there is no need for the dwelling to consist of a house or even a self-contained flat with full facilities such as a kitchen and bathroom. It is possible for a single room bed-sit to be a 'dwelling house' within the meaning of the Act even if the occupant shares the use of facilities outside the bed-sit with others. In the case of *Uratemp Ventures Ltd v Collins* (2001) HLR 85 the House of Lords held that accommodation consisting of one room can be regarded as a separate dwelling as long as the occupant had exclusive possession of it and it could properly be considered to be the occupant's home.

3.2.3 Residence

Under the HA 1988 in order for a tenancy to be an assured the tenant, or at least one them in the case of joint tenants, must occupy the property as his 'only or principal home' (s 1(1)(b) of the HA 1988). It makes no difference in this context whether or not the tenancy is assured or assured shorthold. Physical presence is not necessary so long as the tenant evinces some intention to return to the property by, for instance, leaving his furniture there (*Crawley BC v Sawyer* (1987) 20 HLR 98, CA). For example a tenant who ceased to reside in the dwelling because he or she had been admitted to hospital would probably retain his assured status but a tenant who entered long-term residential care probably would not. Where the landlord has established that the tenant has left the premises it is for the tenant to prove a continuing intention to return. The evidence must objectively demonstrate that intention. Evidence of the tenant's subjective intentions will not suffice. The requirement is the same as that imposed on public sector tenancies by s 81 of the HA 1985 and cases decided under that section may be of assistance. Cases decided under the RA 1977 will be of limited assistance as the residency requirement under that Act is less strict.

3.3   Tenancies which are not assured

Tenancies granted before the 1988 Act came into force are not assured tenancies (para 1 of Sch 1); nor are new tenancies granted to Rent Act tenants of the same premises as they occupied prior to the commencement date of the HA 1988 (s 34 of the HA 1988). In addition Sch 1 to the HA 1988 excludes the following tenancies from the Act's provisions:

Tenancies under which the annual rent exceeds £25,000 (para 2). The extent to which a landlord could limit the tenant's security of tenure by including in the tenancy agreement provisions to change the rent so as to deprive the tenant of protection has been the subject of academic speculation but little judicial authority until the case of *Bankway Properties v Penfold-Dunsford* (2001) *The Times*, 24 April 2001. The Court of Appeal decided that a term in an assured tenancy agreement increasing the annual rent to £25,000 2 years after the tenancy commenced was a sham. It had been found as a fact that that provision had only been included to enable the landlord to determine the tenancy when the tenant did not pay. The tenant was on housing benefit and it was known that he would not have the means to pay that figure, which bore no resemblance to what the property was worth in any case. It would seem to follow from this that provisions which enable the landlord to reduce the rent to below the minimum or above the maximum permitted to make a tenancy a protected or assured tenancy will be similarly void, if the court is satisfied that it is a sham.

- Tenancies at no rent (para 2).

- Tenancies at low rent (defined as less than £1,000 in greater London and £250 or less elsewhere (para 3A).

- Business tenancies to which Part II of the Landlord and Tenant Act 1954 applies (para 4).

- Tenancies of licensed premises (para 5).

- Tenancies of agricultural land. However, if the agricultural land is let together with a dwelling house and does not exceed 2 acres the tenancy will not be excluded from the Act (para 6).

- Student lets where the landlord is an educational institution and the tenant is a student at that institution. Only designated educational institutions can avail of this exception.

- Holiday lettings (para 9)

- Lettings by resident landlords (see para 3.4.1).

- Tenancies granted by the Crown.

- Tenancies granted by certain public sector landlords (see para 3.4.2).

3.4 Excluded parties

Certain tenancies will not be assured because of the status of one or other of the parties to the tenancy. Schedule 1 to the Act provides that tenancies granted by resident landlords and public sector landlords are excluded. An important category of excluded tenants are those who have been accommodated in private sector accommodation by local authorities pursuant to their duties under Part VII of the Housing Act 1996 (Homelessness).

3.4.1   Resident landlords

Where the landlord and the tenant occupy separate dwellings within the same building the tenancy under which the tenant occupies may not be assured. Where the tenancy was granted on or after 15 January 1989, it will not be assured if, when the relationship of landlord and tenant first arose between the parties, the landlord's only or principal home was in the same building as the property let (para 2(b) of Sch 1 to the HA 1988). In other words, a landlord cannot deprive his tenant of assured status by moving into a dwelling within the building after the tenancy has commenced. Another flat in a purpose built block will not come within this exception, and there is then still potentially an assured tenancy (para 1(a)). The requirement of residence for a landlord in this context is the same as for a statutory assured tenant (see 3.2.3). The provisions which prevent there being an assured tenancy are dependent on the landlord's continued residence in the building. However, if a resident landlord assigns his interest to another person who then resides in the building, the tenancy will remain unprotected for 28 days (para 17(1)(a)). In that 28-day period, the assignee can either take up residence or serve written notice that he intends to do so within the next 6 months. As long as he takes up residence within 6 months, the notice will serve to prevent there being an assured tenancy. However, during any period when there is no landlord actually resident within the building, the courts can order possession only where grounds have arisen which would allow for the making of such an order against an assured or assured statutory tenant (para 21). There are further provisions which deal with the position where the resident landlord dies and/or his interest is vested in trustees (paras 18–20).

3.4.2   Public sector landlords

Tenancies granted by local authorities cannot be assured and will be secure tenancies under the HA 1985. Some older tenancies granted by housing associations are secure rather than assured, but the vast majority are governed by the HA 1988. Tenants of fully mutual housing associations are neither secure nor assured.

3.4.3   Homeless applicants

Persons who have applied to a local authority for accommodation on the grounds that they are homeless are entitled to be housed on an interim basis while the application is considered (s 188 of the HA 1996). Local Authorities frequently turn to the private sector to secure this accommodation. Such tenancies are not initially assured or assured shorthold but may become so after the period of 12 months beginning with the date upon which the applicant is notified of the local authority's decision (s 209 of the HA 196).

Applicants housed in hostels and/or bed and breakfast accommodation are not tenants and do not have protection of the Protection from Eviction Act 1977 (see *Desnousse v Newham LBC* [2006] 3 WLR 349).

3.5 Assured tenancies with limited security of tenure

A landlord must obtain a possession order from the court if he wishes to regain possession of premises let on any kind of assured tenancy. However, Part 1 of Sch 2 to the HA 1988 lists a number of situations, referred to as 'mandatory grounds for possession', where a landlord will have an unfettered right to an order for possession in proceedings against his assured tenant. This is in contrast to most commonly used grounds for possession, which usually require the court to be satisfied that it is reasonable to make a possession order before it requires the tenant to vacate. Some of these mandatory grounds are dependent on the satisfaction of specified conditions before the grant of the tenancy, usually the service of a particular notice at the commencement of the tenancy. In addition to these assured tenancies with limited protection, the Anti-Social Behaviour Act 2003 introduced the concept of the 'demoted tenancy'. This Act gave certain public sector landlords the right to apply to court to limit the security of tenure of assured tenants who have been guilty of anti-social behaviour.

3.5.1 Ground 1: landlord's own occupation of the premises

Ground 1 applies either where the landlord (or at least one joint landlord) has occupied the premises as his principal home before the beginning of the tenancy or, when possession is being sought, the landlord requires the premises as his or his spouse's principal home. Not later than the beginning of the tenancy, notice must be served on the tenant telling him that the landlord may recover possession pursuant to this ground. The court does, however, have a discretion to waive a failure to serve this notice if it considers it just and equitable to do so.

3.5.2 Ground 2: possession required by a mortgagee exercising a power of sale

Ground 2 applies where a mortgagee, such as a bank or building society, under a mortgage of the property, which was granted before the tenancy, wishes to claim possession to enable him to exercise a power of sale. The Ground is available only where notice was served before the grant of the tenancy. The Act refers to such 'notice ... as mentioned in Ground 1'. It is not clear whether this refers to notice that possession may be recovered pursuant to Ground 1 or to Ground 2 (see Appendix A for a suggested form of notice). Commercial mortgagees would be well advised to, but surprisingly often do not, make the service of such a notice a condition for their giving permission to mortgagor borrowers to grant tenancies.

3.5.3 Ground 3: holiday accommodation

This ground applies where, within the 12 months before the commencement of the tenancy, the dwelling house had been occupied under a right to occupy it for a holiday. The tenancy which is subject to Ground 3 must be for a term certain not exceeding 8 months. Before the tenancy commences, the tenant must be served with written notice telling him that the ground applies and the court does not have discretion to waive service of that notice.

3.5.4 Ground 4: student accommodation

This ground applies where, within the 12 months before the commencement of the tenancy, the dwelling house had been subject to a tenancy which was prevented from being assured because it was granted by a recognised educational institution to a student. The new tenancy must be for a term certain not exceeding 12 months if this ground is to apply. Before the tenancy commences, the tenant must be served with written notice telling him that the ground applies. The court does not have a discretion to waive service of that notice.

3.5.5 Ground 5: accommodation for ministers of religion

This ground applies where a dwelling house is held for the purpose of being available for a minister of religion as a residence from which to perform his duties. The court will grant possession if satisfied that the property is required for that purpose. It is immaterial how long the tenancy subject to this ground was granted for. The court does not have a discretion to waive service of that notice.

3.5.6 Demoted tenancies

The Anti-Social Behaviour Act 2003 inserted a new s 6A and s 20B into the HA 1988. These sections give registered social landlords such as housing associations the power to apply to the county court for an order that a fully assured tenancy be demoted to an assured shorthold tenancy in cases where it is alleged that the tenant or other occupant has been guilty of anti-social conduct. This may be done within possession proceedings and can be sought as an alternative to a possession order. If the landlord does not give notice that it intends to commence possession proceedings within one year of the demotion order being made the tenancy becomes once again assured. If the landlord serves a notice of intention to commence possession proceedings and then either fails to act on it within 6 months or withdraws it the tenancy again becomes assured.

3.6 Security of tenure of assured tenants

Assuming that the assured tenant does not fall under any of the exceptions set out above, he enjoys a reasonable degree of security of tenure. When an assured tenancy comes to an end for example due to the expiry of its fixed term, a periodic tenancy arises by virtue of s 5(2) of the HA 1988. The terms of the new period tenancy will be the same as the old fixed term tenancy. An assured tenancy, whether fixed term or periodic, cannot be ended by the landlord except with a court order for possession. Outside the cases listed above the only mandatory ground that is usually available to a landlord seeking possession is failure to pay rent for 2 months or more. In all other cases involving the tenant's default the court has a discretion as to whether or not to grant a possession order. In practice, this discretion provides the tenant with a reasonable degree of protection as the courts are not usually willing to evict tenants on discretionary grounds save in the clearest of cases. If there is a prospect of the tenant addressing the alleged default the court is more likely to either adjourn proceedings to enable the tenant to do so or to suspend or postpone the operation of any possession order.

3.7 Assured shorthold tenancies

Assured shorthold tenants have very limited security of tenure. Landlords have an automatic right to a possession order as long as they fulfil the procedural requirements.

3.7.1 Prior to 1997

In order to for an assured tenancy to be shorthold it had to be granted for a term certain of not less than 6 months (s 20(1)(a) of the HA 1988). In addition the landlord had to serve a notice in a prescribed form on the tenant prior to the commencement of the tenancy informing him of her that it was to be shorthold. The prescribed form is set out in the Assured Tenancies and Agricultural Occupancies (Forms) Regulations 1997 (SI 1997/194) which is available online at the website of the Office of Public Sector Information (www.opsi.gov.uk). Failure to comply with these provisions meant that landlords frequently granted fully assured tenancies even where they intended to grant a shorthold tenancy only.

3.7.2   Post-1997

Subsequent to the coming into force of the HA 1996 on 28 February 1997 all new assured tenancies are assured shorthold tenancies (s 19A of the HA 1988). The landlord may still grant a fully assured tenancy by the service of a notice to that effect. Alternatively, the tenancy agreement can expressly state that it is to be fully assured. A tenancy which replaces an existing assured (non-shorthold) tenancy will not be a shorthold tenancy unless the tenant serves a notice on the landlord saying it is to be an assured shorthold (para 7 of Sch 2A). The HA 1996 removed the requirement that the tenancy be for a minimum of 6 months. However, the landlord will not be able to recover possession under the shorthold ground until at least 6 months have elapsed since the commencement of the tenancy (s 21(5) of the HA 1988). All subsequent tenancies of the same or substantially the same premises will be deemed to be assured shorthold tenancies, unless the landlord serves a notice on the tenant telling him that is not the case (para 1(2) of Sch 2A to the HA 1996). There is a slightly more effective form of rent control available to tenants under assured shorthold tenancies than where the tenancy is the basic assured tenancy under the HA 1988.

3.8   Succession

On the death of a tenant only resident spouses and civil partners are entitled to succeed to an assured periodic tenancy. A person who was living with the original tenant as if a spouse or civil partner shall be treated as his or her spouse or civil partner (para 2(2) of Sch 4 to the HA 1988 as amended by the Civil Partnership Act 2004). In the rare situation where more than one person was living with the deceased as a spouse, the court is given a power to determine which of them shall succeed to the tenancy (para 2(3) of Sch 4). There can only be one succession to an assured periodic tenancy. Unexpired fixed term assured tenancies devolve according to the tenant's will or the rules of intestacy.

4 Regulated Tenancies

4.1 Introduction

A tenancy under which a dwelling house or a part of one was let prior to 15 January 1989 is a protected tenancy (s 1 of the Rent Act (RA) 1977), and remains so even if subsequently renewed after that date. After the contractual term of a protected tenancy has expired, a statutory tenancy will arise (s 2(1)(a) of the RA 1977). A statutory tenancy can also arise on the death of the protected tenant (s 2(1)(b) of the RA 1977). Unlike other tenancies, a statutory tenancy confers a personal right to remain in the premises only, and does not amount to an interest in the land. The terms of the statutory tenancy will be the same as the terms of the expired protected tenancy (s 3(1)). Both protected and statutory tenancies may be referred to as regulated tenancies (s 18(1) of the RA 1977). Certain types of residential tenancies are, however, specifically excluded from being protected or statutory tenancies under the RA 1977 (see below).

Many pre-Housing Act (HA) 1988 tenancies remain in existence and it remains important for the practitioner to be able to ascertain whether or not a tenancy granted prior to the HA 1988 qualifies for protection under the RA 1977. Rent Act tenancies are subject to rent control. In addition, Rent Act tenancies enjoy a high degree of security of tenure. The presence of a Rent Act protected tenant may therefore have a significant impact on a property's market value.

4.2 Requirements

In order for an occupant to be a protected tenant he has to fulfil certain criteria. Firstly, there must be a tenancy as opposed to a licence (see para 2.3). Secondly, the tenancy must be of a separate dwelling. Additionally, a statutory tenancy will only arise at the end of a protected tenancy if the tenant continues to occupy the dwelling as his residence and if the if the tenant is an individual. Thus a company may be a protected tenant but cannot become a statutory tenant at the end of the fixed term.

4.2.1 Let as a separate dwelling

The first consideration is whether the property in question constitutes a separate dwelling. The test is the same as that contained in s 1(1) of the HA 1988 and the same principles apply (see para 3.2.2). However, if by the terms of the tenancy the tenant has exclusive occupation of part of his accommodation but shares accommodation with persons other than the landlord then the tenancy may still be regulated (see s 22(1) of the RA 1977). Further, the parties must have intended that the property would be used by the tenant as a dwelling and not for some other purpose (*Russell v Booker* (1982) 263 EG 513). Thus a tenant cannot claim the protection of the RA 1977 simply by moving into the premises and occupying them as his residence if they were initially let to him to be used as for the purpose of carrying out a business (see *Tan v Sitkowski* [2007] 1 WLR 1628).

4.2.2   Residence

A statutory tenancy will only arise at the end of a protected tenancy if the tenant occupies the dwelling as his residence (s 2(1) of the RA 1977). If the tenant ceases to so occupy the dwelling he ceases to be a statutory tenant. The Act does not, however, effectively define 'residence'. A tenant can have more than one residence (cf the HA 1988 where the tenant must occupy the premises as his only or principal home). The residence must be by the tenant personally: the fact that a member of his family lives there will not suffice (cf *Richards v Green* [1983] 268 EG 443, where the tenant always intended to return, and *Brickfield Properties v Hughes* [1988] 20 HLR 108, CA, where the intention to return was merely contingent). Residence is a question of fact and degree. It is possible for a person to have more than one 'residence' (*Brickfield Properties*). Merely sleeping at a property for several nights a week will not necessarily make it one's residence (*Hampstead Way Investments v Lewis-Weare* [1985] 1 WLR 164, HL). The courts should have regard to whether the tenant carries on the majority of life's activities, such as eating, cooking, bathing and socialising as well as sleeping at the property (*Kavanagh v Lyrondias* [1985] 1 All ER 560, CA). A temporary absence, even an extended one, will not result in a cessation of residence (*Tickner v Hearn* [1960] 1 WLR 1406; *Richards v Green*, above). However, where the tenant spends most of his life abroad he will not be able to claim to be resident in the premises (*DJ Crocker v Johal* [1989] 42 EG 103, CA). A tenant who leaves premises under duress will not be deemed to have ceased to occupy it as his residence unless it can be shown that he has found a new home elsewhere, as opposed to temporary refuge (*Raye v Kerr* [2006] HLR 21).

4.3 Excluded tenancies

As with the HA 1988 a tenancy may not benefit from the protection of the RA 1977, notwithstanding the fact that it fulfils the statutory requirements, if it falls into one of the excluded categories.

4.3.1 Business tenancies

A tenancy cannot be a regulated tenancy if it is a tenancy to which Part II of the Landlord and Tenant Act 1954 applies (s 24(3) of the RA 1977). The 1954 Act will apply to any tenancy where the demised premises, or part of the demised premises, are occupied by the tenant for the purpose of carrying on a business. A tenancy will not acquire regulated status merely because the tenant has ceased all business activity on the premises and occupies it only as his residence (see *Tan v Sitkowski* above).

4.3.2 Dwelling houses above certain rateable values

Generally, properties with rateable values on 1 April 1973 (or when it was first valued, if later) in excess of £750 (£1,500 in Greater London) cannot be subject to protected tenancies. Rates were not abolished until after the RA 1977 was repealed (at least in respect of new tenancies), so old rateable values are still relevant. The only exception is where the value did not exceed specified amounts when the property was first valued or other amounts during the revaluation in the spring of 1973 (s 4 of the RA 1977). In practice few rented properties exceeded these values.

4.3.3 Tenancies at low rents

A tenancy is not a protected tenancy if no rent is payable, or if the rent payable is less than two-thirds of the rateable value of the property on the 'appropriate day' (s 5(1) of the RA 1977). The appropriate day will be 23 March 1963 unless the property was first valued on a later day, in which case it will generally be the day it was first valued (s 25 of the RA 1977). In the rare situations where a Rent Act tenancy is granted after 1 April 1990 a tenancy will be a tenancy at low rent for these purposes if the rent is less than £1,000 per annum in greater London and £250 elsewhere. In practice this monetary exception is of little significance as it is difficult to imagine that a tenancy at such low rents would be in existence even in 1977.

4.3.4 Dwelling houses let with other land

If a dwelling house is let with other land to which it is merely an adjunct, there will not be a protected tenancy (s 6 of the RA 1977). However, unless the other land consists of more than 2 acres of agricultural land, it will be taken as part of the dwelling house and will not prevent there being a protected tenancy (s 26 of the RA 1977).

4.3.5 Payments for board and attendance

Where a part of the rent for which a dwelling house is let is bona fide payable in respect of board or attendance, there will not be a protected tenancy (s 7(1) of the RA 1977). Board, which is the provision of meals, must be more than minimal if the tenancy is not to be protected. Provision of continental breakfast will suffice (*Otter v Norman* [1988] 2 All ER 897, HL), whilst merely providing hot drinks would probably not. Attendance includes personal services, such as cleaning and making beds. Services provided by a landlord in respect of common parts of a building do not constitute attendance, eg cleaning heating, etc. For the tenancy not to be protected, the sum fairly attributable to the attendance, having regard to the value of the attendance to the tenant, must form a substantial part of the whole rent (s 7(2) of the RA 1977). This provision was one that was sometimes used by landlords wishing to avoid the Rent Acts.

4.3.6 Lettings to students

A tenancy granted by a specified educational institution to students while they study will not be a protected tenancy (s 8 of the RA 1977).

4.3.7 Holiday lettings

A tenancy is not a protected tenancy if its purpose is to confer on the tenant the right to occupy the dwelling house for a holiday (s 9 of the RA 1977).

4.3.8 Agricultural holdings

A tenancy is not a protected tenancy if the dwelling house is comprised in an agricultural holding and is occupied by the person responsible for the control of the farming of the holding (s 10 of the RA 1977). These tenancies are subject to the control of the Agricultural Holdings Act 1986 and associated legislation.

4.3.9   Licensed premises

Where a tenancy of a dwelling house consists of or comprises premises licensed for on-sales of alcohol, there will not be a protected tenancy (s 11 of the RA 1977).

4.3.10   Resident landlords

A tenancy of a dwelling is not regulated where the dwelling forms part only of a building and the landlord resides in another part (s 12 of the RA 1977). As with assured tenancies this exception does not apply where the building in question is a purpose built block of flats. Where the landlord was resident in the same premises as the tenant, there would usually be a restricted contract under the RA 1977. However, a restricted contract is deemed to end on the first date there is a change in the rent and a new contract arises. If the rent is changed on a date after 15 January 1989 a new tenancy is deemed to arise which will be either an assured or an assured shorthold tenancy depending on the circumstances (see Chapter 3). For this reason the law relating to restricted contracts is now for practical purposes obsolete.

4.3.11   Landlord's interest belonging to Crown, local authority, housing association or co-operative

There will not be a protected tenancy where the landlord's interest is held by the Crown (s 13 of the RA 1977), local authority (s 14 of the RA 1977), housing association (s 15 of the RA 1977) or housing co-operative (s 16 of the RA 1977). Each of these is defined in the appropriate section.

4.4   Company lets

Only an individual is capable of 'residing' in a dwelling house. Therefore, if a property were let to a company, there would be no statutory tenancy (*Hiller v United Dairies (London) Ltd* [1934] 1 KB 57). A 'company let' could, however, be a protected tenancy during the contractual term and the fair rent provisions would then apply (*Carter v SU Carburettor Co* [1942] 2 KB 288). Sometimes, landlords insisted on prospective tenants forming a company so that premises can be let to them without there being the possibility of a statutory tenancy. Although this device sometimes succeeded (see, for example, *Firstcross Ltd v East West (Import/Export) Ltd* [1980] 255 EG 355, CA), there was a danger that the tenant company will be deemed to have sub-let to the actual occupier, notwithstanding any prohibition against that which may appear in the tenancy agreement. The courts would not allow the device of a 'company let' to succeed if doing so would be giving effect to a pure sham. On the other hand, the mere fact that there has been an attempt to avoid the Rent Acts will not automatically lead the courts to treat an agreement as a sham (*Hilton v Plastile Ltd* [1989] 5 EG 94, CA). Further if premises are let to a limited company for the purpose of securing a tax advantage for that company there will be no sham even though all parties knew that the premises were to be occupied by an individual as his residence (*Eaton Square Properties Ltd v O'Higgins* [2000] EGCS 118).

4.5 Protected shorthold tenancies

This type of tenancy, introduced by the HA 1980, enabled a landlord letting property under a tenancy that was otherwise protected to be sure of being able to reclaim possession when the contractual term came to an end. Case 19 of the RA 1977 effectively deprived the shorthold tenant of all non-contractual security of tenure. Such a tenancy had to be for a fixed term between 1 and 5 years and could not to contain a clause entitling the landlord to re-enter prior to its termination except if the tenant is in breach of an obligation of the tenancy (s 52(1)(a) of the HA 1980). The landlord must have given the tenant notice that the tenancy is to be a protected shorthold tenancy before it was granted (s 52(1)(a) and (3) of the HA 1980). If the tenancy would be a shorthold one but for the landlord's failure to serve the proper notice, the court has a discretion to treat it as a shorthold tenancy in a possession action if it is just and equitable in all the circumstances to do so (s 5(2) of the HA 1980). An existing regulated tenancy with full security of tenure could not be converted into a shorthold tenancy by the parties entering into a new shorthold tenancy agreement (s 52 of the HA 1980). No new protected shorthold tenancies are capable of being granted after 15 January 1989.

4.6 Succession

As a statutory tenancy is a personal right to occupy a property, rather than a proprietary right, it will cease to exist upon the death of the statutory tenant. However, when a protected or statutory tenant dies, the landlord is not always entitled to possession of the premises. If the spouse or civil partner of the original tenant survives him and is living in the premises at the time of his death, s/he shall be entitled to remain in the premises as a statutory tenant (paras 1 and 2 of Sch 1 to the RA 1977). If the date of death is after 15 January 1989 a person who lived with the tenant as if a spouse/civil partner will also be entitled to succeed under this provision. If there is no spouse, any other member of the tenant's family who lived with him in the premises for the 6 months prior to his death may become either a statutory or assured tenant depending on the date of death (para 3 of Sch 1). If there is a dispute amongst various family members over who should become the new tenant, the matter should be referred to the county court. There can only be two successions to a regulated tenancy. The rules on succession differ depending on whether the deaths of the original tenant and/or of the first successor took place before 15 January 1989, the date of the entry into force of the HA 1988 and are contained in Part 1 of Sch 1 to the RA 1977. In short, the date of the death of the original tenant and the first successor can alter both the requirements for succession by a family member and whether the tenancy to which he or she succeeds is regulated or assured.

4.7 Recovering possession

The circumstances in which a landlord may recover possession of premises let under a regulated tenancy are specified in Parts 1 and 2 of Sch 15 to the RA 1977. If the court is satisfied that circumstances specified in Part 1 (Cases 1–10) arise, the court may make a possession order. These are the discretionary grounds for possession and the court will only make an order for possession if it considers it reasonable to do so. Where the circumstances specified in Part 2 to Sch 15 to the RA 1977 (Cases 11–20) arise, the court must make a possession order. These are the mandatory grounds for possession, many of which are dependant on the service of a specific notice at the commencement of the tenancy.

4.7.1 Case 1: non-payment of rent or breach of other term of tenancy

This case applies where any rent due from the tenant has not been paid or the tenant has been in breach of any other legally enforceable term of the tenancy. Courts are normally reluctant to order possession on the grounds of arrears of rent alone if there is any realistic prospect of the arrears being paid off. A common course is to make a possession order and suspend its operation for so long as a prescribed amount of the arrears and all future payments are regularly made.

Where there is a forfeiture clause and the tenant's default, for instance going bankrupt, brings that clause into operation, that will be treated as a breach of the terms of the tenancy for the purposes of this case. It does not matter that going bankrupt was not specifically otherwise prohibited by the tenancy agreement (*Cadogan Estates v MacMahon* [2000] 4 All ER 897, HL).

4.7.2   Case 2: nuisance or illegal use of premises

This case applies where the tenant, anyone residing with him or a sub-tenant has been guilty of a nuisance or causing annoyance to adjoining occupiers or has been convicted of using or allowing the dwelling to be used for immoral or illegal purposes.

4.7.3   Case 3: waste

This case applies where the condition of the dwelling has deteriorated due to acts of waste (neglect) by the tenant or anyone living with him. The case will also apply if such acts have been committed by anyone who is a lodger or a sub-tenant, but only if the tenant has not taken reasonable steps to remove that person.

4.7.4   Case 4: deterioration of furniture

This provision is the expressed in similar terms to Case 3 where the condition of the furniture in the premises has deteriorated due to ill-treatment.

4.7.5   Case 5: tenant's notice to quit

This case applies where the tenant has given notice to quit and, in consequence, the landlord has taken steps that would result in him being seriously prejudiced were possession not granted. This case is rarely relied upon, but it is hard to see a court refusing possession if the landlord had entered into an unconditional contract to sell or re-let the premises in reliance on a tenant's intention to go.

4.7.6   Case 6: sub-letting by tenant

This case applies where the tenant has, without the consent of the landlord, sub-let or assigned the whole of the dwelling.

4.7.7   Case 7: employees' accommodation

This case applies where the tenant was let into possession of the dwelling as a term of his employment with the landlord or a former landlord and that employment has ceased. To take advantage of this case, the landlord must also establish that he now requires the premises as a dwelling for someone engaged in his full time employment. This case does not apply to agricultural employees.

4.7.8   Case 8: property required by landlord

This case applies where the dwelling is reasonably required by the landlord as a residence for himself, his children who are over 18, his parents or his parents-in-law. This does not apply if the landlord became such by purchasing the property unless the purchase was before a date specified in the case, the latest of which is 24 May 1974. (Becoming landlord by purchase must be distinguished from purchasing the property and then becoming landlord, which does not prevent this case applying.)

4.7.9   Case 9: overcharging sub-tenants

This case applies where the tenant sub-lets all or part of the premises at a rent which is in excess of the registered fair or reasonable rent (if any and as appropriate) for that part of the premises.

4.7.10   Case 10: owner-occupiers

For Case 10 to apply, certain conditions have to have been satisfied before the tenancy is granted. If these have been satisfied and if the landlord has served the requisite notice on the tenant prior to the commencement of the tenancy the landlord will be entitled to possession. The court may waive the requirement of prior written notice if is just and equitable to do so. The conditions to be satisfied are laid down in Part V of Sch 15 to the RA 1977. These are:

(a)   the dwelling is required as residence for the landlord or any member of his family who resided with him when he last occupied the dwelling as a residence;

(b)   the landlord has died and the dwelling is required as a residence for a member of his family who resided with him at the time of his death;

(c)   the landlord has died and the dwelling is required by a successor in title as a residence or for the purpose of selling it with vacant possession;

(d)   the dwelling is subject to a mortgage made by deed before the granting of the tenancy, and the mortgagee is entitled to exercise a power of sale and requires the dwelling in order to dispose of it with vacant possession pursuant to that power; and

(e)   the landlord wishes to dispose of the property with vacant possession and use the proceeds to buy a residence which is suitable for his needs having regard to his place of work, which the dwelling let is not.

4.7.11   Case 11: retirement homes

The primary requirement of this case is that the landlord intends to occupy the dwelling house as his residence at such time as he might retire from regular employment and has let the property before retiring. The requirements as to notice in respect of this and any previous tenancies of the property the landlord may have granted are the same as for Case 10 tenancies, and the court has a similar discretion to override these requirements. The court must be satisfied that the owner has retired and requires the dwelling house as a residence (Part 5 of Sch 15 to the RA 1977).

4.7.12   Case 12: holiday accommodation

This case applies where, within the 12 months before the commencement of the tenancy, the dwelling house had been occupied under a right to occupy it for a holiday. The tenancy which is subject to Case 12 must be for a term certain not exceeding 8 months. Before a tenancy subject to this case commences, the tenant must be served with written notice telling him that the case applies and the court does not have discretion to waive service of that notice.

4.7.13   Case 13: student accommodation

This case applies where, within the 12 months before the commencement of the tenancy, the dwelling house had been subject to a tenancy which was prevented from being protected by s 8(1) of the RA 1977 because it was granted by a recognised educational institution to a student. The tenancy subject to this case must be for a term certain not exceeding 12 months. Before a tenancy subject to this case commences, the tenant must be served with written notice telling him that the case applies. The court does not have a discretion to waive service of that notice. It is unlikely that there are any of the inherently transient tenancies covered by this provision still in existence.

4.7.14   Case 14: accommodation for ministers of religion

This case applies where a dwelling house is held for the purpose of being available for a minister of religion as a residence from which to perform his duties. The court will grant possession if satisfied that the property is required for that purpose. It is immaterial how long the tenancy subject to this case was granted for. Before the commencement of the tenancy the tenant under this case had to be served with written notice telling him that the case applied. The court does not have a discretion to waive service of that notice.

4.7.15   Cases 15, 16 and 17: agricultural accommodation

These cases apply where the dwelling house has, at some time, been occupied by an agricultural employee under the terms of his employment and the current tenant has never been employed by the landlord and is not the widow of a person who was so employed. The court will grant possession if satisfied that the dwelling house is required for occupation by an agricultural employee of the landlord. Before the relevant date the tenant under this case has to have been served with written notice telling him that the case applies. The court does not have a discretion to waive service of that notice.

4.7.16   Case 18: protected shorthold tenancies

This case applied where the tenancy granted was a protected shorthold tenancy. To obtain possession, the landlord had to follow the procedure which is prescribed within the case and proceedings had to be started within 3 months of the service of the appropriate notice seeking possession. The notice must have been served, at the latest, 9 months from the date of expiry of the tenancy. For this reason this case is for practical purposes obsolete.

4.7.17   Case 19: accommodation owned by members of the armed forces

For this case to apply the landlord must have been a member of the regular armed services both at the date when he acquired the property and also when the tenancy was granted. Further conditions must be satisfied at the time possession is sought. He must have served the appropriate notice on the tenant before the commencement of the tenancy and must not have granted any tenancies in respect of which such a notice was not served since acquiring the property. The court, however, has a similar discretion to waive the service of this notice as it does for Case 10.

4.7.18   Suitable alternative accommodation: s 98

A court may make a possession order if it is satisfied that suitable alternative accommodation is available for the tenant, or will be when the possession order takes effect. This alternative accommodation may be, but does not need to be, provided by the landlord. Rules about what may constitute suitable alternative accommodation are set out in Part 4 of Sch 15. A certificate from a local authority that it will provide suitable alternative accommodation will be conclusive on that question (para (3)). However, even once accommodation is found to be suitable, whether because of the authority's certificate or otherwise, the court still has a discretion whether or not to order possession. The court will take into consideration the security of tenure of the proposed alternative accommodation when considering the issue of reasonableness and the availability of rent control.

4.7.19   Overcrowded dwellings: s 101

Where a dwelling is overcrowded, the provisions which prevent a landlord from recovering possession are suspended. 'Overcrowded' is defined in Part 10 of the HA 1985. A dwelling will be overcrowded if there are not sufficient rooms for every occupant over the age of 10 not to have to share a bedroom with someone of the opposite sex unless they are living with that person as husband and wife (s 325 of the HA 1985). There are also minimum permissible sizes for the rooms people occupy (s 326). The material date for the purposes of this section is the date of trial, so if occupants have left the dwelling between the commencement of proceedings and trial, resulting in it no longer being overcrowded, the tenant will be entitled to the usual statutory protection. The fact that a landlord is in breach of his covenant by allowing the premises to become overcrowded will not defeat a possession claim brought under this section (*Buswell v Goodwin* [1971] 1 WLR 92, CA).

4.8   Possession procedure

Unlike proceedings under the HA 1988 there is no need for the landlord to serve a statutory notice on the tenant before bringing proceedings. However, the landlord would be best advised to informally notify the tenant in writing of the fact that he intends to start proceedings for possession and of the grounds upon which he intends to rely. The court will not grant an order unless it is satisfied that the protected tenancy has come to an end, either by service of a valid notice to quit in the case of a periodic tenancy or by effluxion of time or forfeiture in the case of a fixed term tenancy. Those regulated tenancies which still exist are likely to be statutory tenancies rather than protected tenancies.

The general procedure for obtaining a possession order is set out in Chapter 8. The court has the same powers of suspension, adjournment and postponement as it would have in cases involving assured tenancies (s 100 of the RA 1977). As with assured tenancies the courts power to suspend an order or adjourn the hearing are severely limited when the landlord has established a mandatory ground for possession.

5 Rent and Other Payments

5.1 The obligation to pay rent

The amount of rent payable under any tenancy is primarily a matter for the parties to that agreement. Residential tenancies do not constitute an exception to that principle: landlord and tenant are free to agree any rent that they wish. However, where the Rent Act (RA) 1977 applies, either party has a right to ask an independent body to assess a fair rent in the case of a protected or statutory tenancy. Once such a rent has been assessed, the contract between landlord and tenant is overridden to the extent that that rent becomes the maximum payable. Where the Housing Act (HA) 1988 applies and there is an assured tenancy, there is no right to apply for a rent to be assessed on the initial granting of the tenancy, although there is such a right where there is an assured shorthold tenancy. The tenant may ask for the rent to be independently assessed on the renewal of the tenancy if the landlord wishes to increase it.

5.2 Regulated tenancies

The body with initial jurisdiction to assess a fair rent under the RA 1977 is the Rent Service and the person who assesses the rent is referred to as the rent officer. The functions of the rent service were transferred to the Valuation Office Agency in May 2009. The parties' right to apply to the Rent Service to assess a binding 'fair rent' in respect of the demised property cannot be excluded by any prior agreement between the landlord and tenant (s 44(2) of the RA 1977). The application can be made by either a protected or statutory tenant. Fair rents have historically been below market rents; sometimes, particularly in London, dramatically so. However, these reduced values were due to the fact that prior to the passing of the HA 1988 there was virtually no free market in residential rented property. Since that Act came into force, there has been a gradual increase in the rents assessed by rent officers, rent assessment committees and courts (see *Curtis v London Rent Assessment Committee* [1999] QB 92). The relevant legislation is contained in Part IV, ss 62–75 of the RA 1977. The government attempted to introduce regulations that would mitigate the harshness of these increases for tenants by capping the increases (Rent Acts (Maximum Fair Rent) Order 1999 (SI 1999/6)). Despite a powerful argument, accepted in the Court of Appeal, that these

Regulations were *ultra vires*, their validity was confirmed by the House of Lords in *R v Secretary of State for the Environment ex parte Spath Holme Ltd* [2001] 1 All ER 195.

5.2.1 The Rent Service's jurisdiction

The Rent Service only has jurisdiction to assess a rent if there is a tenancy and it is 'regulated' within the meaning of s 18 of the RA 1977. The fact that there is not a tenancy capable of becoming a 'statutory' tenancy because, for instance, the tenant is not resident (see para 4.2.2) or is not an individual will not affect the Rent Service's jurisdiction. If the Rent Service's jurisdiction is challenged by a party (most commonly this will be by the landlord claiming there is a licence rather than a tenancy), the rent officer may still determine a fair rent if he thinks it appropriate to do so (*R v Rent Officer for Camden ex p Ebiri* [1981] 1 All ER 950). If the rent officer is not willing to do so, the party making the application can apply to the county court for a determination of whether or not the tenancy is regulated (s 141 of the RA 1977). Such an application should be made using the procedure set out in Part 8 of the Civil Procedure Rules.

5.2.2 Procedure for the assessment of a fair rent

Section 67 of the RA 1977 provides that the application for the assessment of a fair rent can be made by the landlord, the tenant or both jointly. The application must be on the prescribed form (s 67(2) of the RA 1977) which is available online on the Valuation Office Agency website www.voa.gov.uk. Completion of the form is very straightforward. It is essential that the question asking what amount of rent the applicant is seeking to register be answered. If this is not done, the application will be void (*Chapman v Earl* [1968] 2 All ER 1214). To avoid prejudicing their position, landlords are generally best advised to state what they believe to be the market rent (perhaps that presently being charged) and leave it to the rent officer to decide how much it has to be reduced. For similar reasons, tenants often state an unrealistically low amount, such as £20 per week.

After receiving the application, the rent officer can ask either party to provide further information. At the request of either party or at his own volition the rent officer can hold a meeting for the parties, at which they can be represented by counsel, a solicitor or anybody else. The rent officer will listen to any arguments concerning the amount of rent that should be registered. Factors such as the size and condition of the premises can be referred to. Any particularly onerous or unusual terms in the tenancy agreement should be drawn to his attention.

The rent officer may ask to inspect the premises prior to assessing the rent payable. The amount of the fair rent that the rent officer has determined will then be notified to the parties and registered.

5.2.3 Appeals against the Rent Service's assessment

An appeal against the Rent Service's decision is by way of a full rehearing of the application before the Rent Assessment Committee. This is a separate body from the Rent Service and is now part of the Residential Property Tribunal Service. Such an appeal must be made within 28 days of the notification of the rent officer's decision to the parties. The appeal is made by writing to the Rent Service giving notice of objection to his decision The Rent Service will then refer the matter to the Residential Property Tribunal Service. A notice of appeal received after the 28-day period may still be entertained if either the rent officer or the Rent Assessment Committee exercise their discretion to do so (para 6(1) of Sch 11 to the RA 1977). The committee has a power similar to that of the rent officer to request further information from either party (para 7(1) of Sch 11 to the RA 1977). Non-compliance with a request of the committee without reasonable excuse is a criminal offence punishable by a fine (para 7(2) of Sch 11 to the RA 1977). Usually, the committee will inspect the premises and hold an oral hearing. They must hold the hearing if either party requests it (para 8 of Sch 11 to the RA 1977). The committee may either affirm the rent officer's decision or set a fair rent of their own (para 9(1) of Sch 11 to the RA 1977). The committee could vary the rent upwards even if it were the tenant who appealed and downwards even if it were the landlord, a fact to which the attention of a party considering an appeal should always be drawn. There is a right of appeal to the High Court on a point of law against the committee's decision (s 11 of the Tribunal and Inquiries Act 1992). Rent assessment committees, like rent officers, are also subject to the supervision of the High Court by way of judicial review and must give reasons for their decisions (see *R (on the application of Woltors (London) Ltd v London Rent Assessment Committee & Ors* [2003] 41 EG 180).

5.2.4 Effect of registering a fair rent

The consequence of the registration of a fair rent is that no greater amount of rent may be recovered by the landlord in respect of those premises (ss 44 and 45 of the RA 1977). Where the fair rent is more than the contractual rent, the landlord may not increase the rent during the contractual term of the tenancy: paradoxically, an increase, though not a decrease, is regarded as a breach of the tenancy contract. Once the contractual term has expired, he may increase the rent up to the amount of the fair rent, but must serve a notice of increase (s 45(2)(b) of the RA 1977). This notice must be in the prescribed form (for which see the Rent Act 1977 (Forms etc) Regulations 1980 (SI 1980/1697)) (s 49(2) of the RA 1977). It may be served during the contractual period even though it relates to the following statutory tenancy (s 49(3) of the RA 1977). A fair rent is effective only from the date on which it is first registered unless the rent is eventually determined by a rent assessment committee, when it is effective only from the date of their decision (s 72(1)(b) of the RA 1977). It is therefore in the interests of the party hoping to benefit from the application to proceed as quickly as possible. If the application is the tenant's, it would not be exceptional for his rent to be halved. During the inevitable delay before the committee hears the appeal, he will have to continue paying the existing rent. This extra payment may cancel out any benefit he would gain from a reduction in the assessed rent, even if his appeal succeeds.

An application to vary the fair rent may be made at any time by either party on the basis that the circumstances appertaining to the property and/or the tenancy have changed so as to make the rent previously assessed no longer fair (s 67(3) of the RA 1977). Otherwise, the tenant may not apply for a new rent until 2 years have expired since the last registration. The landlord may apply after 21 months, although the new rent will not become effective until after the expiry of the 2-year period (s 67(4)).

5.2.5 Factors taken into account in the determination of a fair rent

The legislation does not provide the Rent Service and the Rent Assessment Committee with any formulae to use in assessing the amount of fair rent to be registered. They are merely told to have regard to all the circumstances (other than personal circumstances) and, in particular, to the age, character, locality and state of repair of the dwelling house and, if any furniture is to be provided for use under the tenancy, the quantity, quality and condition of the furniture (s 70(2) of the RA 1977). Any scarcity of either would-be tenants or (far more significantly) property available for letting is to be disregarded (s 70(2)). Assured tenancy comparables may be taken into account, though the rent office must not lose sight of the fact that security value will not have been disregarded in respect of them. It is not improper for a rent officer to disregard them altogether, though it will become increasingly impractical to do so (*Spath Holme Ltd v Greater Manchester and Lancashire Rent Assessment Committee* [1995] 49 EG 128, CA).

The best way to find out roughly how much a fair rent is likely to be in respect of any property is to consult the public register retained by the Rent Service. The rents registered recently in respect of comparable dwellings in the same area will give a fair indication of the probable figure. A list of the most recent assessments can be found online on the website of the Valuation Office Agency - www.voa.gov.uk.

5.3 Rent control for assured tenancies

5.3.1 Initial rent

The HA 1988 allows a landlord to charge whatever rent he is able to negotiate when a tenancy is first granted. This rent will remain payable so long as the initial contractual assured tenancy lasts. The 1988 Act is based on the free market principle of allowing the parties to strike their own bargain. Once the initial contractual term expires, the tenant may be entitled to remain as a periodic statutory tenant. The landlord is entitled to carry on receiving the same rent during that tenancy unless he wishes to increase the rent.

5.3.2 After the expiry of the fixed term

There is nothing to prevent a landlord and tenant from agreeing an increase in the rent payable (s 13(5) of the HA 1988). Further s 1(1)b of the HA 1988 provides that if the tenancy agreement contains a rent review clause which makes provision for the rent to be increased the statutory framework of rent control has no application. In the event that the parties do not agree a rent increase or there is no rent review clause in the agreement, the procedure for increasing rent is contained in s 13 of the HA 1988. The landlord may not increase the rent until the tenancy has lasted for at least 12 months, though he may serve notice of increase within that period (s 13(2) of the HA 1988). The notice of increase, in which the landlord 'proposes' a new rent, must be served on the tenant so as to expire after that 12-month date. In the case of a yearly tenancy, at least 6 months' notice must be given, otherwise a period of notice equal to the period of the tenancy must be given, subject to a minimum period of one month (s 13(3) of the HA 1988). The notice must be in the prescribed form otherwise it will not be valid and the rent increase will not take effect (see the Assured Tenancy and Agricultural Occupancies (Forms) (Amendment) (England) Regulations 2003 (SI 2003/260)). The form can be viewed on the website of the Office of Public Sector Information (www.opsi.gov.uk). The rent increase proposed in the notice will then take effect automatically unless the tenant refers the matter to a Rent

Assessment Committee or persuades the landlord not to impose the increase (s 13(4) of the HA 1988). Many tenants do not appreciate the significance of the notice and will fail to take advantage of their right to refer it to the committee, thus allowing their rent to be increased by default.

5.3.3 Reference of a proposed rent increase to a rent assessment committee

The reference to the committee must take place before the notice of proposed increase has expired, otherwise the committee will have no power to consider it. The application must be made on the prescribed form which is available from the Residential Property Tribunal Service's website – www.rpts.gov.uk.

The committee determines the rent to be charged after the expiry of the notice of increase with reference to the rent they consider that the dwelling house concerned might reasonably be expected to be let in the open market by a willing landlord under an assured tenancy (s 14(1) of the HA 1988). The committee, in making that evaluation, is to assume that the hypothetical tenancy is for the same period and on the same terms (except for rent) as the tenancy they are actually considering. However, the committee is to disregard the effect on rent of the tenancy being granted to a sitting tenant, who might be prepared to pay 'over the odds' to preserve his home and also any extra-contractual improvements carried out by the tenant or deterioration caused by his failure to comply with the tenancy agreement (s 14(2) of the HA 1988). There is a significant contrast with the corresponding provisions under the RA 1977 in that the committee is not required to disregard any effect that scarcity of similar rented accommodation has on the amount of market rent. Normally, the rent decided upon by the committee will be backdated to the date of expiry of the notice (assuming they have been unable to assess it before that date). There is, however, a discretion where the tenant would otherwise be caused 'undue hardship' to postpone the coming into effect of the increase until any date up to that of the actual assessment.

5.4 Rent control in respect of assured shorthold tenancies

Where an assured shorthold tenancy is granted, the tenant has a right to make an application to the rent assessment committee to determine the rent. The committee will be able to consider the application only if it considers there are a sufficient number of similar dwelling houses in the same locality (s 22(3)(a) of the HA 1988). The committee will consider whether the contractual rent is significantly higher than the rent which the landlord might reasonably be expected to obtain having regard to the level of rents paid under similar tenancies in the locality. The application has to be in the prescribed form (s 22(1) of the HA 1988) which again is available on the Residential Property Tribunal Service's website – www.rpts.gov.uk. The rent assessed by the committee, if different from that charged by the landlord, shall be payable from such date as the committee may determine. It may not, however, be backdated to before the date of the application (s 22(4)(a) of the HA 1988). The statute does not seem to envisage the possibility of the committee determining a rent higher than the contractual rent. However, if such a rent were determined, there is nothing in the section that would enable a landlord to recover any amount over and above his contractual entitlement. An application may not be made for a determination of rent if the rent payable under the tenancy has already been determined by a rent assessment committee (s 22(2) of the HA 1988). If there is an assured shorthold tenancy granted after the commencement of the HA 1996, no application may be made after more than 6 months after the commencement of that tenancy (s 22(2)(aa)). No application may be made if the parties have entered into a new tenancy agreement upon the expiry of the initial tenancy, or if the tenant remains in occupation under a statutory periodic tenancy (s 22(2)). Once a rent has been determined under this provision, the landlord may not serve a notice of increase of rent until at least 12 months after the determination (s 22(4)(c) of the HA 1988).

5.5   Notification of the landlord's address

Section 47 of the Landlord and Tenant Act 1987 requires landlords to state their name and address on any rent demand sent to tenants. If the landlord is not resident in England or Wales, the demand must also state an address at which notices, including notices in proceedings, can be served on the landlord. Section 48 of the 1987 Act further requires the landlord to provide the tenant with a notice giving an address in England or Wales at which notices can be served on him. If these provisions are not complied with, no rent or service charge is due from the tenant until the address is supplied (ss 47(2) and 48(2)). If a landlord fails to comply with this section on the grant of the tenancy but later remedies his default any sums which were not payable due to the landlords breach of this requirement will fall due on service of the notice. An unqualified statement of the landlord's address in the tenancy agreement may suffice for the purposes of s 48 (*Rogan v Woodfield Building Services* [1994] EGOS 145, CA). Since the HA 1996 came into force, the tenant can require the landlord to give him written notice of many terms of the tenancy not already reduced to writing (s 20A). This includes the amount of rent, the dates it is payable, provision for rent reviews, and length of the term if it is a fixed term tenancy (s 20A(2)). This provision seems to overlook the fact that a tenancy is supposed to be an agreement between two parties, with neither having more power to impose terms than the other. Although the section does say that the statement by the landlord will not be conclusive proof of the terms, it suggests that landlords should have greater power than basic contractual principles would suggest.

5.6 Other payments

5.6.1 Premiums

Although it was an offence under the RA 1977 to charge a premium for the granting of a protected tenancy, this does not apply to assured tenancies granted under the HA 1988. However, if such a premium is charged, the tenancy then becomes assignable, which is not otherwise the case (s 15 of the HA 1988).

5.6.2 Rent books

Where the rent is payable weekly by a residential occupier, except one for whom board is provided, it is a criminal offence for the landlord not to provide a rent book (ss 4 and 7 of the Landlord and Tenant Act 1985). The book must contain prescribed information (s 5), which is specified in the Rent Books (Forms of Notice) Regulations 1982 (SI 1982/1474). Rent books in the correct form are obtainable from many general stationers. This obligation does not arise if, as is commonly the case, the rent is payable on a monthly basis.

5.6.3 Maximum charges for gas and electricity supplies

Maximum prices, for gas and electricity are specified by the gas and electricity authorities by s 37 of the Gas Act 1986 and s 44 of the Electricity Act 1989. The Landlord may not charge more for gas and electricity than he is charged by the supplier but may include a separate charge for administration. The maximum resale price for gas and electricity is set by the Office of Gas and Electricity Markets (OFGEM) and further information is available at www.ofgem.gov.uk.

5.6.4   Stamp duty

Stamp duty was abolished for the vast majority residential tenancies in 2003 when it was replaced by stamp duty land tax. Broadly speaking the tax is only payable in respect of tenancies where the total rent payable under the agreement exceeds £125,000. Stamp duty is still due in respect of tenancy agreements which were executed prior to 1 December 2003, save where the total annual rent does not exceed £5,000. The court may refuse to accept as evidence a tenancy agreement which has not been duly stamped.

5.7   Deposits

The HA 2004 ushered in a new regime in respect of any deposit payable on the grant of an of assured shorthold tenancy. It applies to tenancies which commenced on or after 6 April 2007. Deposits paid in respect of tenancies which commenced prior to that date are not subject to any specific statutory regime. In the event of a dispute between the parties the only formal remedy available to the tenant is to bring proceedings in the county court for return of any sums which he believes are being wrongly retained by the landlord. There is of course no obligation on a landlord to require payment of a deposit but those that do must now comply with the Act. Upon payment of a deposit the landlord has a choice of two schemes: a custodial scheme whereby the deposit is paid into a designated account until the end of the tenancy, and an insurance scheme whereby the landlord keeps the deposit but enters into a policy of insurance which will repay the deposit to the tenant in the event of the landlord's default. Both schemes have procedures for the resolution of disputes in the event that the parties cannot agree what is to happen to the deposit at the end of the tenancy.

The landlord must comply with the statutory requirements within 14 days of receipt of the deposit. He must also inform the tenant of the details of the scheme which he has chosen and provide the tenant with information as to his rights under that scheme (s 213 of the HA 2004).

The penalties for non compliance with the Act are severe. The tenant may apply to the court for an order compelling the landlord to comply. If the court is satisfied that the landlord has not complied with the Act it must order the landlord to either comply with the Act, or to repay the deposit to the tenant. Additionally, the court must order the landlord to pay the tenant a sum equal to three times the deposit as damages (s 214). Further, the landlord who has required the payment of a deposit may not serve notice seeking possession under s 21 of the HA 1988 on the tenant until he has complied with the Act (s 215).

6 Obligations During the Currency of the Tenancy

6.1 Repairing obligations

The parties to a tenancy agreement are, to some extent, free to agree upon their respective repairing obligations. There is no implied obligation at common law to keep the demised premises in good condition or even to keep them in a condition which is fit for human habitation. The harshness of the common law is tempered by statute which will imply a covenant to repair into most residential tenancies. In addition, local authorities have certain statutory powers which allow them to force landlords to carry out repairs. However, if a dwelling is in poor condition for reasons which the landlord is not obliged to remedy, either by statute or by the terms of the tenancy, the tenant will have no remedy against his landlord. This is so even if the condition of the property significantly interferes with the tenant's ability to live in and generally use the property.

6.1.1 Covenants implied by statute

Section 11 of the Landlord and Tenant Act 1985 implies a covenant to repair in residential leases granted for a period of less than 7 years. This implied covenant obliges the landlord to:

(a) keep in repair the structure and exterior of the dwelling (including drains, gutters and external pipes); and

(b) keep in repair and proper working order the installations in the dwelling for:

the supply of water, gas and electricity and for sanitation; and

for space and water heating (s 11 of the Landlord and Tenant Act 1985).

If the dwelling is a flat the duty contained in s 11 extends to any other part of the building in which the landlord has an estate or interest. Thus the tenant can require a landlord to carry out repairs to the common parts of a building and to keep in repair the installations which serve his flat regardless of whether they are within his demise (s 11(1A)).

The meaning of 'keep in repair' within s 11(1)a does not oblige the landlord to carry out any works would amount to an improvement. The landlord is not required to address problems which are attributable to inherent defects in the building's construction. This can give rise to some odd results. For example a landlord will be liable under this section for dampness caused by a deterioration of an existing damp proof course within the exterior walls of a building, however he would not be liable for dampness caused by the complete absence of a damp proof course. By way of further example in the case of *Quick v Taff-Ely Borough Council* ([1986] QB 809) the Court of Appeal held that a landlord was not liable for severe condensation dampness caused by the poor design of the property in question, despite the fact that the condensation was so bad as to render that property unfit for human habitation.

The structure of a dwelling consists of those elements of the overall dwelling which give it its essential appearance, stability and shape (*Irvine v Moran* [1991] EGLR 261). It will usually extend to the exterior and interior walls, the floors and ceilings, and the doors windows and roof. It will not extend to the interior decoration. However, if the internal decorations become damaged due to the presence of disrepair or as a result of the execution of repairs, the landlord is obliged to 'make good' the damage (*Bradley v Chorley Borough Council* (1985) 17 HLR 305).

This covenant cannot be excluded by agreement between the landlord and tenant, although there is a little used power for the parties to make a joint application to the court for an order varying or excluding it (s 15 of the Landlord and Tenant Act 1985).

A landlord only becomes liable under this covenant once he has been given notice of the disrepair (*Al Hassani v Merrigan* [1988] 3 EGLR 88, CA). The landlord will only be liable if he fails to carry out repairs within a reasonable time after he has notice. The requirement of notice does not apply where the part of the building that is in disrepair is a part that the landlord has retained (*Passley v London Borough of Wandsworth* (1996) 30 HLR 165).

6.1.2 Liability for defective premises

Section 4 of the Defective Premises Act 1972 obliges landlords who are under a repairing obligation to take such care as is reasonable to ensure that all persons who could reasonably be expected to be affected by defects in the demised premises are safe from personal injury or damage to property. It is to be noted that this duty extends to visitors to the premises and is not limited to the tenant. The duty is owed in relation to defects of which the landlord is aware or about which he ought reasonably to have known (s 4(2)) In *Sykes v Harry* ([2001] QB 1014), the Court of Appeal held that a landlord was liable for injury caused by a defective gas heater even thought he was not aware of the fact that the heater was defective. The landlord in question had not had the heater inspected for some years and ought to have realised that there was a significant risk that it had become defective. The duty extends to damage caused by a 'relevant defect', defined as a defect which the landlord would be under a duty to repair if he had notice of it (s 4(4)). The duty extends to items of disrepair which the landlord has a right to enter to repair, and not just to those items of disrepair which he is obliged to repair under the terms of the tenancy (*McAuley v Bristol City Council* [1992] QB 134). The landlord is not liable for any injury caused by a defect for which the tenant is responsible (s 4(4)).

6.1.3   Powers of the local authority

The Environmental Protection Act 1990 gave local authorities far reaching powers to force landlords to address hazards to health and disrepair in rented residential property. These statutory powers were revised and strengthened by the Housing Act (HA) 2004. The local authority may inspect rented premises to check for hazards. If a serious hazard (category 1) is identified the local authority must take action to see that the hazard is addressed. The local authority may take action if the hazard is deemed to be less serious (category 2). The local authority may serve an improvement notice on the landlord requiring him to remove the hazard or, in cases of urgency the local authority may take emergency remedial action and recoup the cost from the landlord. The landlord may appeal to the Residential Property Tribunal Service if he is dissatisfied with the decision of the local authority.

A complaint to the local authority may be the only remedy available to a tenant where his dwelling is in poor condition but that condition is not due to any breach by the landlord of a repairing covenant. Common problems which will not usually be covered by the landlord's repairing covenant are pest infestations and mould growth caused by condensation dampness.

6.1.4   Remedies for landlord's breach

A tenant can bring an action against his landlord seeking specific performance of a repairing covenant. The tenant may also claim damages. The damages can be calculated by reference to a notional diminution in the rent for the period during which the disrepair existed. Alternatively, the court can make a global award based on the discomfort and inconvenience caused to the tenant. In the case of *Wallace v Manchester City Council* (1998) 30 HLR the Court of Appeal referred to, but did not expressly approve, an 'unofficial tariff' of awards of between £1,000 per annum and £2,500 per annum (which updated amounts to a tariff of between £1,325 and £3,320). If the tenant carried out the repairs himself, then he can recover the cost from his landlord.

The tenant does not have an automatic right to withhold rent because of a breach of repairing covenant by the landlord. However, a claim for damages arising out of such a breach can be treated as an equitable set off in any claim by the landlord based on rent arrears (*British Anzani (Felixstowe) Ltd v International Marine Management (UK) Ltd* [1980] QB 137). Landlords frequently seek to exclude such the right of set off by including a covenant within the lease obliging the tenant to pay the rent 'without any deduction or set off whatsoever'. However, it is likely that a clause in a standard form tenancy agreement which seeks to limit the tenants rights in the event of the landlords breach would be deemed to be 'unfair' within the meaning of the Unfair Terms in Consumer Contracts Regulations 1999 (SI 1999/2083) and thus unenforceable against a tenant. These regulations will apply to residential tenancies where the parties use the supplier's (in this case the landlords) standard form of agreement (see *London Borough of Newham v Khatun* [2005] QB 37). In practice, therefore, most residential tenants will be able to rely on the landlord's failure to repair as a partial defence to any claim based on rent arrears.

6.1.5 Remedies for tenant's breach

If it is the tenant who is in breach of a repairing covenant, the landlord is entitled to damages. These damages may not exceed the amount by which the value of the landlord's reversionary interest has been reduced due to the breach (s 18(1) of the Landlord and Tenant Act 1927). The breach may also form a ground on which the court may order possession under Case 1 of Sch 15 to the Rent Act 1977 or Ground 12 of Sch 2 to the HA 1988.

There is also an implied obligation on the tenant not to commit acts of waste (damage or destruction). Breach of this will entitle the landlord to damages and potentially to possession under Case 3 or Ground 13.

Breach of a repairing covenant may also entitle a landlord to forfeiture of the lease during its contractual term. However, the procedure for forfeiting a lease on this ground is cumbersome and is usually only used in cases involving long residential leases (ie leases granted for 21 years or more). For disrepair to premises let on shorthold tenancies the landlord is best advised to simply bring possession proceedings based on s 21 of the HA 1988 and seek damages if appropriate.

6.2   Gas regulations

Under the Gas Safety (Installation and Use) Regulations 1998 (SI 1998 No. 2451) landlords have to take considerable steps to ensure the safety of their tenants where there are gas appliances owned by the landlord in the premises. The main duty on the landlord is the obvious one: not to install a gas appliance unless it can be used without constituting a danger to any person. Every year, the landlord must ensure that every gas appliance in the property is checked for safety by an approved person. This means, in effect, someone who is registered on the Gas Safe Register (formally CORGI). The landlord must also keep a record in respect of each gas appliance stating any defects identified and any remedial action that has been taken in respect of that defect. The landlord should keep some proof of each such inspection. An itemised receipt should be sufficient. Most gas safe registered engineers will be prepared, for a small additional charge, to issue a formal certificate of safety. This is probably only necessary for landlords who have a large number of properties and find difficulties keeping records or where there is a history of conflict with the tenants.

Any tenant who might be affected by a gas appliance is entitled to inspect the record which relates to it on giving the landlord reasonable notice. Landlords are under a duty to provide the tenant with a copy of the details of the inspection within 14 days of its being carried out, whether or not the tenant actually requests it. In the case of a new tenancy, the landlord will have to provide the tenant with a copy of the inspection record before the tenant moves in.

It is a defence for the landlord to show that he took all reasonable steps to comply with the Regulations, but was unable to do so. A landlord who employs a contractor to go to a property, notifies the tenants when the contractor is coming, and who is not told by the tenants that the time is inconvenient, would probably have a defence if the contractor was not admitted by the tenants to the property.

A gas appliance for these purposes is one 'designed for use by a consumer of gas for heating, lighting, cooking, or other purposes'. This will include boilers and other central heating devices as much as it does fires.

Responsibility for the enforcement of the regulations lies with the Health and Safety Executive. Failure to comply with the regulations can result in a fine and/or imprisonment. A failure which results in the death of a tenant can lead to a charge of manslaughter. In 2007, a landlord was sentenced to 2 years' imprisonment when his failure to have a gas boiler checked properly led to the death of his tenant through carbon monoxide poisoning.

6.3   Furniture regulations

The Furniture and Furnishings (Fire) (Safety) Regulations 1988 (SI 1988/1324, as amended by SI 1989/2358 and SI 1993/207) require landlords to comply with the same regulations as regards the provision of fire resistant furniture as currently apply to retailers. All furniture supplied under tenancies has to:

(a)   have upholstery that complies with the 'cigarette test'. This is a test carried out according to a British Standard specification, designed to ensure that the furniture will not burst into flames when a cigarette is dropped on it. Beds, including mattresses and pillows, are exempt from this requirement;

(b)   have a filling that complies with further 'ignitability tests';

(c)   have any permanent covers that pass the 'match test'.

Furniture which satisfies these requirements will be labelled accordingly. Second-hand shops and auctioneers should no longer sell furniture that does not comply with these Regulations. The tenant may require a landlord to replace any items of furniture which do not comply with the Regulations.

6.4   The tenant's right to occupy and enjoy the property

6.4.1   The right of quiet enjoyment

At common law, there is an implied term that the tenant is entitled to 'quiet enjoyment' of the demised premises. The landlord is obliged not to do anything that will detract from the rights the tenant has been granted. The most serious breach of this covenant is wrongful eviction of the tenant. It is a criminal offence for a landlord to unlawfully evict a residential occupier (whether or not a tenant) (s 1 of the Protection from Eviction Act 1977). If the tenant is unlawfully evicted, his first course of action, if he wishes to return, should be to seek an injunction compelling the landlord to re-admit him to the premises.

The covenant to allow quiet enjoyment also applies so as to prohibit less drastic interferences with a tenant's rights. Such actions as cutting off services, deliberately allowing the premises to fall into a state of disrepair, and even forcing unwanted sexual attentions on a tenant, give the tenant a right to take action for breach of this covenant. The mere withholding of normal 'social intercourse', even if that is to be expected by reason of the proximity in which the landlord and tenant live, cannot constitute a breach of this covenant: *Morris v Knight* (1999)

CLY 3682. The fact that the landlord's behaviour was not motivated by a desire to force the tenant out does not affect the tenant's right to an injunction and/or damages, although the tenant would then be less likely to receive exemplary damages (see para 6.4.2).

An unlawful interference with the rights of occupation of a tenant or licencee will usually constitute an offence pursuant to s 1 of the Protection from Eviction Act 1977. Section 2 of the Act obliges the owner of residential property let on a tenancy to obtain a court order before enforcing his right to possession. This protection also extends to licences (s 3(2B)). Certain categories of tenancy and licence are excluded from the Act's protection. These are set out in s 3A. The main category of excluded licences and tenancies are those where the tenant shares his accommodation with the landlord or with a member of the landlord's family. In addition, licences granted by a local authority to occupy hostel accommodation are usually excluded from the Act's protection (see para 3.4.3).

6.4.2 Damages for interference with the right to quiet enjoyment

At common law an illegally evicted tenant is entitled to damages, either in addition to or instead of an injunction. The normal measure of damages is the value of the loss of the tenancy. In practice, the monetary value to the tenant of an assured shorthold tenancy is likely to be nominal unless the terms of the tenancy were very favourable to the tenant. If the eviction has been carried out in a particularly unpleasant manner, for instance violently, the tenant may be entitled to aggravated damages to compensate for the additional distress this has caused him. The court may also award exemplary damages where the landlord has been motivated by the belief that he would make a profit from his actions even after paying the tenant damages (*Drane v Evangelou* [1978] 1 WLR 455, CA). The tenant may claim for any extra expenditure which the unlawful eviction has caused him to incur. He may also claim for any damage to his belongings directly caused by the eviction.

6.4.3 Damages for wrongful eviction under the HA 1988

The HA 1988 introduced an elaborate scheme for the assessment of damages to be awarded to illegally evicted tenants. This scheme exists concurrently with the right to claim damages at common law for tort or breach of contract, though a tenant will not be able to recover damages on both bases in respect of a single claim (s 27(5) of the HA 1988). The Act provides that a residential occupier will be entitled to damages where he gives up his right to occupy the premises as a consequence of various specified acts done by his landlord with the intention of causing the occupier to give up the premises or refrain from exercising rights in respect of them (s 27). These acts include anything calculated to interfere with the peace or comfort of the occupier or his household or a persistent withdrawal or withholding of services reasonably required for the occupation of the premises (s 27(2)). The measure of damages to be awarded to an occupier who gives up the premises in those circumstances is the difference between the value of the landlord's interest in the building in which the premises are contained, with and without the occupier in occupation (s 28). In determining the value of the landlord's interest once the occupier is no longer present, it will be assumed that it is unlawful to redevelop the property (s 28(3)). However, if the occupier is reinstated in the premises before the commencement of proceedings, he will lose his right to damages under the Act (s 27(5)). Such an occupier may still have a valid claim at common law.

Damages under this section have been awarded against a landlord who, having obtained a possession order, enforced it himself, but without first obtaining a warrant from the court (*Haniff v Robinson* [1993] QB 419, CA). The highest reported award under this provision was £46,500 in *Tagro v Cafane* [1991] 1 WLR 378, CA.

The importance of the tenant's statutory right to damages under s 27 has declined in recent years. This is because most tenancies are now assured shorthold. These have limited effect on a property's market value due to the ease with which an assured shorthold tenant can be evicted. However, the presence of tenant with a higher degree of security of tenure can have a significant effect on the market value of a property and consequently damages under this section could be substantial.

7 Ending the Tenancy

7.1 Introduction

Historically, residential tenants have had a considerable degree of protection from landlords who wished to regain possession of the demised property. The Rent Act (RA) 1977 perhaps represented the high point of the tenant's position in this respect. The protection was substantially eroded by the Housing Act (HA) 1988 and then by the amendments made by the HA 1996. The procedure by which a landlord regains possession of his premises let on any kind of assured tenancy begins with the service of a notice. The function of the notice is twofold: firstly, it informs the tenant of his landlord's intention to go to court to regain possession; and, secondly, it informs him of the ground(s) upon which the landlord intends to rely.

As far as the landlord is concerned the common law/contractual methods of termination are of little relevance when dealing with an assured tenancy. Indeed, these tenancies may only be terminated by the landlord with an order of the court (s 5 of the HA 1988). However, the common law methods of termination are still relevant when dealing with tenancies which are excluded from the protection of the HA 1988 or which have, for whatever reason, lost their assured status. Additionally, an assured tenant may still avail himself of the common law or contractual methods of termination if he wishes to bring his tenancy to an end.

7.2 Common law methods of termination

7.2.1 Effluxion of time

At common law a fixed term tenancy will automatically come to an end at the end of the agreed term; there is no need for either party to serve notice on the other. Because an assured tenant may avail of the common law methods of termination he may simply move out of the premises at the end of the tenancy. There is no need to notify his landlord of his intention to do so. However, the landlord who wants to regain possession at the end of an assured shorthold tenancy is best advised to serve a s 21 notice on the tenant if he wishes to be certain of regaining possession (see para 7.3). If after the term has ended the tenant retains exclusive possession with the consent of the landlord and continues to pay rent, the court may infer an intention to create a periodic tenancy, unless the surrounding circumstances indicate a different intention on the part of either the landlord or the tenant. If the fixed term tenancy was assured, a statutory periodic tenancy automatically arises at the end of its term if the tenant remains in occupation.

7.2.2 Surrender

Surrender of a lease can be described as the return of the tenant's interest in the property to the landlord by mutual consent. Historically, surrender can be either be by deed (express surrender), or more commonly by implication from the words of conduct of the parties (surrender by operation of law), the latter being by far the most common. The parties can expressly agree that the tenant is to relinquish his tenancy. Alternatively, such an agreement can be inferred by their conduct. The kinds of conduct which will give rise to an inferred surrender on the part of the tenant include returning the keys to the landlord or simply abandoning the premises. The landlord may then simply accept the surrender by retaking possession of the premises. If it is the landlord who alleges that the tenancy has been surrendered then in practice there is no need for him to prove that he accepted it. However, if it is the tenant who alleges that there has been a surrender of the tenancy he must show that the landlord had accepted the surrender (*Bellcourt Estates v Adesina* [2005] 2 EGLR 33). This can be done either by proving the landlord's express agreement to the surrender, or by showing that the landlord subsequently acted in a way which was inconsistent with the continuation of the tenancy, such as re-letting the premises to a new tenant. Surrender of a tenancy will not determine any sub-tenancy granted by the tenant. Further, a joint tenant cannot surrender the tenancy without the agreement of the other joint tenant(s). The tenant's obligations under the tenancy, including the obligation to pay rent, will continue unless and until the landlord agrees to accept the tenant's surrender (*Reichman v Beveridge* [2007] 8 EG 137).

7.2.3 Notice to quit

At common law the landlord or tenant may bring a periodic tenancy to an end by service of a valid notice to quit. By s 5 of the Protection from Eviction Act 1977 a landlord's notice to quit must be in writing and contain certain prescribed information (see Appendix A, para 1.7). In addition, the notice must give the occupant at least 4 weeks' notice. In the case of a periodic tenancy the notice must end on the correct day this being the last day of a period of the tenancy. If it does not then it will not be valid and the tenant will have a complete defence to possession proceedings based on the invalid notice. A joint tenant may serve a notice to quit even though the other joint tenant(s) may not consent to or even be aware of the fact that such a notice has been served (*Hammersmith and Fulham LBC v Monk* [1992] AC 478). Such a notice will operate to determine the tenancy.

7.2.4   Service of the notice

The notice can be served in any of the usual ways: personally, by leaving it at the premises so that it will come to the tenant's attention, or by post. Service on one joint tenant will constitute service on all of them, (*Hammersmith and Fulham LBC v Monk*, above). However, it would be wise to serve notice on all joint tenants, in case difficulties arose in proving that a particular one of them had been served. Similarly, in cases where there are two or more landlords a notice to quit can be validly served by one of them. It may be that the tenancy agreement provides a particular method for service, for example postal service on the premises. Many written tenancy agreements expressly incorporate s 196 of the Law of Property Act 1925 which provides that any notice will be deemed to be lawfully served if it is left at the let premises or at the tenant's last known residential or business address, or is sent by recorded delivery at his last known business or residential address and is not returned undelivered.

7.2.5   Forfeiture

A landlord may have a right to treat the lease as terminated if the tenant is in breach of covenant. In most cases this right is only available if it is expressly included within the terms of the tenancy. The right to forfeit a lease for breach of covenant is subject to substantial statutory restrictions. The law relating to forfeiture is of little relevance to most short residential tenancies as it is far easier to regain possession by relying on one of the statutory grounds for possession provided in the HA 1988.

7.3   Ending an assured shorthold tenancy

7.3.1   Notice seeking possession

The first step in bringing an assured shorthold tenancy to an end will usually be the service of a notice seeking possession under s 21 of the HA 1988. Unlike a notice to quit served on a non-assured periodic tenancy, the s 21 notice does not operate to terminate the tenancy; it is merely the first step in obtaining possession. The notice does not have to be in any particular form but it must be in writing and it must contain the information prescribed by the section. (For specimen notices see Appendix A, paras 1.8 and 1.9.) In cases where a deposit has been paid the landlord may not serve a s 21 notice until the landlord has complied with the statutory requirements for the protection of deposits (see para 5.7).

The right to rely on s 21 as a ground for possession is in addition to any other right to possession the landlord may have (s 21(1) of the HA 1988). Thus the landlord of premises let on an assured shorthold tenancy may rely on any of the grounds for possession set out in Sch 2 to the HA 1988 should he wish to do so.

If at the possession hearing the court is satisfied that the landlord is entitled to rely on s 21 of the HA 1988 then it must make a possession order. It has no power to adjourn the hearing and its powers to delay possession are strictly limited (see *Poplar Housing & Regeneration Community Association v Donoghue* [2001] 3 WLR 183).

7.3.2 When to serve the notice

A s 21 notice may be served at any time during the tenancy. It can be served at the same time as the tenancy agreement is entered into. However, the order for possession can only be made after the fixed term of the tenancy (if any) has ended. The HA 1988 does not prescribe any particular method of service and the same rules apply as those governing service of a notice to quit (see para 7.2.1).

7.3.3 Form and content of the notice

The HA 1988 does not prescribe any particular form of notice. However, it stipulates that the notice must be in writing and must give the tenant at least 2 clear months' notice of the landlord's intention to regain possession. The landlord cannot issue proceedings until after expiry of the notice (*Lower Street Properties v Jones* [1996] 28 HLR 877). If the notice is served during the fixed term it must simply give the tenant at least 2 clear months' notice (s 21(1)(a)). If the notice is served in respect of a periodic tenancy it must additionally state that possession of the premises is required after a date which is the last date of a period of the tenancy (s 21(4)(a)). In practice, this has tended to cause difficulties for the inexperienced landlord. For example in the case of *Fernandez v McDonald* [2003] 4 All ER 1033 the landlord sought to recover possession of premises let on a tenancy which had commenced on 4 September. After this tenancy expired it was replaced automatically with a monthly periodic tenancy by operation of s 5(2) of the HA 1988. The landlord served a s 21 notice which expired on 4 January. This was held to be invalid by the Court of Appeal because the last day of the period of the tenancy was the 3rd of each month, not the 4th. In the premises the notice was one day too long and was therefore invalid as it did not comply with s 21(4)(a). In view of the difficulties in identifying the correct expiry date, the practice developed of including a 'catch all' clause within s 21 notices which stipulated that the possession would be required after the last day of the period of the tenancy which next expired 2 months following service of the notice. Such catch all expiry clauses are valid even if they do not identify a specific expiry date (see *Notting Hill Housing Trust v Roomus* [2006] 1 WLR 1375).

7.3.4 Tenancies which commenced prior to 28 February 1997

For those tenancies which were in existence prior to 28 February 1997 it will also be necessary to show that the landlord served written notice in the prescribed form on the tenant informing him that the tenancy was to be shorthold (s 20 of the HA 1988). This notice must be in the prescribed form and must be given to the tenant before he enters into the tenancy agreement. In practice, courts have tended to accept that this section was complied with if the tenant was given the s 20 notice at the same time as he was given the tenancy agreement for signature (see *Bedding v McCarthy* [1993] 27 HLR 103).

7.4 Ending an assured tenancy

In order to regain possession of premises let on an assured tenancy the landlord will have to establish that one of the grounds set out in Sch 2 to the HA 1988 is made out. The process begins with service of a notice under s 8 of the HA 1988. The s 8 notice must set out precisely which ground is relied upon and the particulars of how it is alleged that the ground is satisfied. Again, service of the notice does not operate to terminate the tenancy; it is merely the first step which the landlord must take if he wishes to bring the tenancy to an end. An order for possession based on service of a s 8 notice may take effect at any time; the landlord need not wait until after the expiry of the fixed term, in contrast to an order based on s 21.

7.4.1 Form and content of the notice seeking possession

The tenant must be given written notice that the landlord intends to start possession proceedings and the ground(s) to be relied upon must be specified within it. The s 8 notice must be in the prescribed form set out in the Assured Tenancies and Agricultural Occupancies (Forms)

Regulations 1997 (SI 1997/194) (see Appendix A, para 10). The form can be viewed on the website for the Department for Communities and Local Government (www.communities.gov.uk). Only 2 weeks' notice need be given unless one or more of Grounds 1, 2, 5–7, 9 and 16 is relied upon, when the period is 2 months. Since the coming into force of the HA 1996, proceedings can be commenced as soon as the notice is served if Ground 14 (nuisance) is relied upon (s 8(4) of the HA 1988). The court, however, has a discretion to dispense with this notice if it considers it just and equitable to do so unless possession is sought in reliance on Ground 8 (rent more than 2 months/8 weeks in arrears) (s 8(1)(b) of the HA 1988).

The notice need not set out the statutory grounds verbatim, though in practice it would be advisable to do so. A notice claiming possession on the basis of Ground 8 was held invalid because of the omission of words to the effect that that ground only applied if there had been the requisite arrears both at the date of the notice and the date of the hearing (*Mountain v Hastings* [1993] 25 HLR 427).

7.5 Mandatory grounds for possession

If the court is satisfied that a mandatory ground for possession is made out it must make a possession order. The courts powers of adjournment are very limited and cannot be used to defeat the purpose of the Act. Thus the court may adjourn the proceedings if it cannot hear the case due to time restraints, or at the request of a defendant who cannot attend and who claims to have a valid defence. In claims based on rent arrears it cannot adjourn the hearing to allow a defendant time to reduce the arrears below the mandatory threshold (see *North British Housing Association v Matthews* [2005] 1 WLR 3133).

7.5.1 Ground 1: landlord has resided or wishes to reside in the property

Ground 1 applies where the landlord has occupied the property as his principal or only home and/or now requires it for himself or his spouse as their only or principal home. A landlord who has bought the property during the current tenancy is not entitled to rely on this ground. There are no restrictions relating to the reasons for which a landlord who has resided there previously now requires possession. The landlord should have served notice of his intention to recover possession under this ground when the tenancy was originally granted. The notice requirement can be dispensed with if the court considers it just and equitable to do so. A landlord who has not resided there previously will merely have to prove that he requires the property as his or his spouse's only or principal home.

7.5.2   Ground 2: possession required by mortgagee

Ground 2 applies where a mortgagee under a mortgage of the property which was granted before the tenancy wishes to claim possession to enable him to exercise a power of sale conferred on him either by the mortgage or by s 101 of the Law of Property Act 1925. Again, there is a requirement either that the tenant was given notice of the possibility of possession being obtained under this ground or that the court thinks it just and equitable to dispense with the notice requirement.

7.5.3   Grounds 3, 4 and 5: lettings of holiday accommodation, lettings by educational establishments and lettings of property intended for ministers of religion

Grounds 3, 4 and 5 apply to out-of-season holiday lets, lettings by recognised educational institutions and lettings of property intended for and now required by ministers of religion. In respect of Grounds 3 and 4, the landlord does not have to show anything other than that the appropriate notice was correctly and justifiably served before the tenancy commenced. The original tenancy must not have been longer than 8 months in the case of Ground 3 and 12 months in the case of Ground 4. In respect of Ground 5, it is also necessary to show that the property is now required for occupation by a minister of religion.

7.5.4   Ground 6: demolition or reconstruction of premises

Ground 6 applies where the landlord intends to carry out substantial work on the property, including demolition or reconstruction, which it is not practicable to do with the tenant *in situ*. This ground is not available where the landlord (or, if there are joint landlords, any of them) bought his interest during the currency of the present tenancy. If the tenant is willing to agree to a variation of the terms of his tenancy, including accepting a tenancy of just part of the property, so as to allow the work to be carried out, the landlord will not be entitled to possession. This provision seems for the most part to be designed to give landlords a lever to persuade tenants to agree to redevelopment, rather than actually lead to possession orders. If possession is ordered pursuant to this section, the court will order the landlord to pay a sum equal to the tenant's reasonable removal expenses (s 11 of the HA 1988).

7.5.5　Ground 7: tenancy passing by will or intestacy

Ground 7 applies where the periodic tenancy has passed by will or intestacy on the death of the former tenant. The landlord can commence proceedings under this Ground in the 12 months thereafter. If he did not know of the former tenant's death at the time it occurred, the 12-month period may, in the court's discretion, start to run from when he found out about it. It is the actual commencement of proceedings, not the service of a s 8 notice, that is relevant for this purpose (*Shepping v Osada* [2000] 2 EGLR 38, CA). The ground expressly declares that the acceptance of rent by the landlord after the former tenant's death does not create a new tenancy. This merely states the position at common law, but nonetheless removes an issue which seems to cause many practitioners much unnecessary worry. This ground applies only where the tenancy has passed by will or on intestacy, rather than under the statutory succession provisions.

7.5.6　Ground 8: 2 months' arrears of rent

Ground 8 applies where the landlord commences proceedings on the basis that at least 2 months' rent (in the case of monthly tenants), or 8 weeks (in the case of a tenancy where rent is paid weekly or fortnightly) is in arrears. If rent is paid quarterly or yearly, at least one quarter's rent must be more than 3 months in arrears. These arrears must exist both at the time the notice seeking possession is served and at the date of the hearing. The provision makes no allowance for the situation when arrears have accrued due to no fault of the tenant's, perhaps through the failure of a local authority to pay housing benefit. As noted above the court may not adjourn the proceedings to permit the tenant to reduce the arrears to below the mandatory threshold (see *North British Housing Association Ltd v Matthews* [2005] 1 WLR 3133). Theoretically, this ground could apply even if the arrears have accrued due to the landlord deliberately avoiding receipt of payment. In those circumstances, the rules of equity may protect the tenant. In *Bessa Plus plc v Lancaster* [1997] EGCS 42, the Court of Appeal held that the landlord was entitled to possession after rejecting payments from the tenant's cohabitee. This decision was made on the basis that she had not tendered the payment as the tenant's agent, and thus suggests that, had she been acting as his agent or had the payment come directly from him and then been rejected, possession would not have been ordered pursuant to this ground.

7.6 Discretionary grounds for possession

Part II of Sch 2 of the HA 1988 contains the discretionary grounds for possession. The court will only order possession on these grounds if it considers it reasonable to do so (s 7(4) of the HA 1988). The court itself must be satisfied that it is reasonable to make the order; the parties cannot by consent agree that it is reasonable.

7.6.1 Ground 9: suitable alternative accommodation available

This ground applies where suitable alternative accommodation is available for the tenant. 'Suitable alternative accommodation' is defined in Part III of Sch 2. Where a local housing authority has certified that such accommodation will be available to the tenant, that will be conclusive (para 3(2) of Part III of Sch 2). Otherwise, the court will have to decide whether the property is suitable for the tenant, having regard to the needs of the tenant and his family and proximity to place of work. The property must also either be similar to that provided by local housing associations for people in similar circumstances to the tenant, or be reasonably suitable for the tenant and his family having regard to extent and character (para 3(1)). If there is a furnished tenancy, the furniture provided in the alternative accommodation must also be similar if the accommodation is to be deemed suitable. Although the schedule expresses itself as defining the concept of suitable alternative accommodation, in most cases it will have left open the factual question of suitability for the court to decide. Where the court makes an order for possession pursuant to this ground it will order the landlord to pay the tenant a sum equal to his reasonable expenses likely to be incurred in moving (s 11 of the HA 1988).

7.6.2 Ground 10: rent arrears

Ground 10 applies where there are some arrears of rent, both when proceedings are begun and when the notice of intention to commence proceedings was served on the tenant. In practice, this ground will usually overlap with Grounds 8 and 11.

7.6.3 Ground 11: persistent delay in paying rent

Ground 11 applies where 'the tenant has persistently delayed paying rent that has become lawfully due'. The draftsman seems to have deliberately left open the question of when exactly a landlord will be able to rely on this Ground. On a strict reading, the reason for the non-payment will be irrelevant: all that matters is whether or not it has occurred persistently. In practice, the courts take a broader view of the provision. In practice, a court will not make a possession order unless there some arrears outstanding as at the date of the hearing, notwithstanding any past poor payment record.

7.6.4 Ground 12: breach of terms of the tenancy

Ground 12 applies where the tenant has been in breach of a term of the tenancy other than payment of rent.

7.6.5 Grounds 13, 14 and 15: waste, nuisance or illegal use of premises and deterioration of furniture

Grounds 13, 14 and 15 apply where the tenant has caused the condition of the dwelling house to deteriorate; where the tenant has been guilty of conduct which is a nuisance to adjoining occupiers; and where the tenant has caused damage to furniture provided under the tenancy. A wider Ground 14 applies since the passing of the HA 1996, where the misbehaviour of the tenant or anyone else residing in, or visiting, the dwelling house causes nuisance to anyone residing in, or carrying on a lawful activity in the locality of, the dwelling. The court, in considering whether to make an order, should have regard to local public opinion on the matter. In *West Kent Housing Association v Davies* (1999) 31 HLR 415, the Court of Appeal reversed a judge's decision not to make an order despite finding that the tenant had caused a nuisance by repairing old cars at the premises and been racially abusive and threatening to neighbours. This ground will also apply if an arrestable offence is committed in, or in the locality of, the dwelling house. The fact that a tenant has been convicted of dealing drugs from the premises will usually lead to an outright possession order being granted, although this his not an automatic presumption (*Sandwell MBC v Hensley* (2008) HLR 22). Section 9A of the HA 1988 (as amended by the Anti-Social Behaviour Act 2003) requires the court to specifically consider the effect that the behaviour has had on other people in the locality and the effect that it will have on such people in the future when deciding whether or not to make an order for possession.

7.6.6 Ground 16: employee tenants

Ground 16 applies where the letting was in consequence of the tenant's employment by the landlord and that employment has ceased. A claim on this basis need not be adjourned because the tenant has made an application to the employment tribunal seeking reinstatement (*Whitbread West Pennines Ltd v Reedy* [1988] ICR 807, CA).

7.6.7 Ground 17: tenancy obtained by a false statement

Ground 17 will apply if the tenant or anyone acting on his behalf obtained the tenancy by recklessly or knowingly making a false statement. It is most likely to be used where something is done to conceal the true identity of the tenant from the landlord.

7.6.8 Ground 14A: domestic violence

Ground 14A applies only where the landlord is a registered social landlord or charitable housing trust. If one partner has been forced out by the other's violence, possession may then be obtained against the remaining partner, regardless of who was the original tenant, but only if the court is satisfied that the non-violent partner is unlikely to return.

7.7 Ending regulated tenancies

As noted in Chapter 4, the RA 1977 does not require the service of a particular notice before the landlord commences possession proceedings against a statutory tenant. However, in order to succeed the landlord must show that the initial protected tenancy has come to an end. Further, it would be wise for the landlord to inform the tenant in writing of his intention to commence possession proceedings and of the grounds upon which he intends to rely. Failure to do so would probably result on an adjournment of the possession hearing.

8 Possession Proceedings

8.1 Introduction

Landlords seeking possession of premises let on a residential tenancy must use the procedure set out in Part 55 of the Civil Procedure Rules (CPR). Part 55 must also be used in possession proceedings against licencees, former licencees, and trespassers. Part 55 of the CPR does not disapply the general rules governing civil litigation; however, it does modify the manner in which the court deals with the proceedings, particularly at the preliminary stage. In particular, it is designed to bring the proceedings before a judge for determination soon after the proceedings are issued. The procedure is designed to take account of the fact that many tenants who wish to defend possession proceedings do not serve a formal defence before this preliminary hearing is listed.

8.2 Commencing proceedings

8.2.1 The claim form

Possession proceedings must be commenced using the prescribed claim form (Form N5) which is available on the Court Service website (www.hmcourts-service.gov.uk). The claim form must be verified by a statement of truth which must be signed by the landlord or his solicitor. Where the landlord is a company it must be signed by a person holding a senior position within the company. A managing agent may not sign a statement of truth on behalf of the landlord (PD 3.11 of Part 22 of the CPR).

The proceedings are formally commenced when the court office issues the claim form. When the proceedings are issued the court will fix an initial hearing date which will be noted on the face of the claim form. The proceedings must be commenced in the county court for the district in which the premises are situated (r 55.3 of the CPR). Proceedings which are commenced in the wrong county court are not invalid but they must be transferred to the correct court before any order can be made. Proceedings commenced using the online procedure (see para 8.9) will be automatically transferred to the correct county court. The vast majority of possession proceedings are commenced in the county court. Proceedings may only be started in the High Court if the proceedings are substantial and complex disputes of fact, points of law of general importance or if the claim is against trespassers and an immediate determination is necessary to avoid public disturbance.

8.2.2 The particulars of claim

The landlord must serve and file particulars of claim with the claim form. In all cases where the landlord is seeking possession of rented residential premises he must use the particulars of claim set out in Form N119 which again is available on the Court Service's website (www. hmcourts-service.gov.uk). The content of the particulars of claim is governed by PD 2.1 of Part 55 of the CPR. However, Form N119 is reasonably self-explanatory. In proceedings which include a claim for non-payment of rent the particulars of claim must additionally set out the amount due at the start of proceedings and include in schedule form all payments made and all payments due since the tenant first defaulted or within the last 2 years if the tenant first defaulted more than 2 years prior to issue. The landlord must also include the daily rate at which rent or interest on rent continues to accrue to the account, and details of any steps which he has taken to recover the arrears. Any known relevant information about the defendant's circumstances must be included within the particular of claim (PD 2.3 of Part 55 of the CPR). The particulars of claim must be verified with a signed statement of truth.

8.2.3 Service of proceedings

Service of proceedings is governed by Part 6 of the CPR. Normally the court will serve the proceedings on the defendant by post (r 6.4 of the CPR). Alternatively, the landlord may chose to serve the proceedings himself in which case the court will return the issued claim form to him for service. The claim form may be served personally on the defendant or posted to or left at his usual or last known address. The claim form will be deemed to be validly served if it is served at the defendant's last known address; the claimant does not have to prove that the defendant actually received the document (see *Akram v Adam* [2005] 1 All ER 741). If the defendant has instructed solicitors to act on his behalf then the proceedings must be served on the solicitors if they are authorised to accept service and the claimant has been made aware of that fact (*Nanglegan v Royal Free Hospital NHS Trust* [2002] 1 WLR 1043). If the landlord decides to serve the proceedings they must be served no less than 21 days before the hearing date (r 55.5(3)(c) of the CPR).

8.3 The preliminary hearing

When the court issues the claim form it will fix a hearing date. This must be no less than 4 weeks and no more than 8 weeks from the date of issue. At this hearing the court may either decide the claim or adjourn it and give directions (r 55.8 of the CPR). The court will usually only adjourn the case with directions if the defendant is seeking to raise an arguable defence to the proceedings.

8.3.1 Practical points

The preliminary hearing will frequently be listed with a large number of other possession actions and the time available to the court for each case may well be limited. In practice, the court will only have time to make possession order in the most straightforward cases. If the case is more complex the court unlikely to have sufficient time to finally dispose of it at the initial hearing unless the claim is unopposed, the facts are uncontested, or the parties are in agreement as to the appropriate order. If the tenant opposes the making of a possession order on grounds which *prima facie* have some substance then the matter will be adjourned to permit him to file a defence. While Part 55 does make provision for the service of a defence prior to the initial hearing, many tenants do not do so, either because they are unfamiliar with the court process or because they have not been able to obtain legal advice beforehand. Because of this Part 55 makes it easier for tenants to file a defence later in proceedings. Thus the landlord may not obtain judgment in default of a defence and Part 10 of the CPR (acknowledgement of service) does not apply (r 55.7 of the CPR). However, the court has the power to penalise the tenant in costs if he does not file a defence within 14 days of service of the proceedings.

8.3.2 Evidence at the preliminary hearing

Rule 55.8(3) of the CPR provides any fact that needs to be proved by witness evidence may be proved by evidence in writing. In straightforward uncontested cases the court may be content for the landlord or his representative to give oral evidence confirming that the contents of the claim form and particulars of claim are true. There ought to be some evidence, either oral or written, confirming service of any requisite notice seeking possession. In most cases it is preferable to serve and file a short witness statement in support of the claim for possession. If the landlord intents to rely on written evidence in support he must serve it at least 2 clear business days before the hearing (r 55.8(4) of the CPR). The statement need not be that of the landlord himself and can be made by a managing agent if appropriate. Landlords are best advised to serve the witness statement as soon as possible. The witness statement need not be particularly detailed but should cover those facts which the must be proved if the court is to be in a position to dispose of the possession proceedings at the first hearing. A sample witness statement is included in Appendix A. The witness statement should deal with the circumstances of the tenancy and the grounds for possession. In addition the witness evidence should also deal with the service of any relevant notice.

Even if a witness statement is served and filed it is advisable to have someone at court on who has knowledge of the day to day management of the tenancy and can assist the court with any queries it may have in relation to the claim.

8.4   The defence

The practice direction to Part 55 of the CPR provides that the defence must be in Form N11 or Form N11R as appropriate. However, these forms are not practical where the defendant wishes to rely on a substantive defence rather than simply bring his personal circumstances to the court's attention. It is common for the defendant to instead file a fully pleaded defence and/or counterclaim. Whichever format is used the defence must be verified with a statement of truth.

A tenant under a contractual tenancy will have a complete defence to a claim for possession if he can show that his tenancy has not been validly terminated. A tenant faced with a claim based on rent arrears may have a defence to the action if he has a counterclaim against his landlord for damages for breach of the duty to repair or any other breach of covenant. A counterclaim will only amount to a defence to the claim for possession if it has some relevance to the ground upon which the landlord relies. Thus the fact that the tenant may have a claim against his landlord for disrepair is no defence to a claim based on nuisance or on s 21 of the HA 1988.

8.5   The powers of the court

At the preliminary hearing the court may dismiss the claim, adjourn the matter with directions or it may make a possession order if it is satisfied that it is appropriate to do so.

8.5.1   Make an order

The court may grant an outright possession order at the preliminary hearing order if it satisfied that the landlord has made out his ground for possession and that the defendant has no prospects of defending the claim. If the court is satisfied that the landlord has established a mandatory ground for possession it must make the possession order. Normally, a possession order will take effect within 14 days of the hearing. The court has the power to extend the delay the date for possession by up to 6 weeks in it is satisfied that the tenant will suffer exceptional hardship (s 89 of the Housing Act 1980). Additionally, the court may give judgment for any outstanding rent arrears. If the tenancy is assured or assured shorthold and the grounds for possession are not mandatory the court may exercise its extended discretion to stay postpone or suspend the possession order (see para 8.7). If the court makes an order on a mandatory ground it ought record this on the face of the order (see *Diab v Counytrwide Rentals* (2001) *Independent,* November 2001).

8.5.2 Give directions

If the court does not dispose of the case and decides instead to give directions it will usually allocate the claim to one of three 'tracks': the small claims track, the fast track or the multi track. Claims for money where the amount in issue is less than £5,000 will normally be allocated to the small claims track. However, if there is a claim against a landlord for damages for harassment or unlawful eviction, the case cannot be allocated to this track (r 26.7 of the CPR) In addition, cases in which a tenant brings a claim for disrepair against his landlord which is likely to exceed £1,000 will not be allocated to the small claims track (r 26.6(1)(b) of the CPR). The main effect of allocation to the small claims track is to restrict the costs which the successful party may recover from the other side (see para 9.2.2).

Most cases in which a possession order is sought will be allocated to the fast track. Cases in which possession is sought can only be allocated to the small claims track if all the parties agree (r 55.9(2) of the CPR. More complex or higher value claims may allocated to the multi track. The fast track is the normal track for cases with a financial value of less than £15,000. There is no limit on the costs which may be recovered on the fast track but the costs which the successful party may recover in respect of the final hearing are fixed by Part 46 of the CPR.

The standard directions which the court will normally give will include the exchange of witness statements, disclosure of documents relevant to the case and the instruction of experts if necessary.

8.6 Extended discretion of the court

Section 9 of the HA 1988 gives the court wide powers to adjourn or stay proceedings as it thinks fit. Further, it gives the court the power to stay or suspend the execution of any possession order or postpone the date for possession at any time up to the execution of the order if it is reasonable to do so. These powers are only available to the court if the tenancy is assured and possession is sought on discretionary grounds only. There is no such extended discretion in cases where the landlord has established a mandatory ground for possession (s 9(6) of the HA 1988). If the court decides to exercise its discretion under this section it will usually impose terms as to the payment of the current rent and the arrears if any, unless it would cause exceptional hardship on the tenant or would otherwise be unreasonable to do so (s 9(3) of the HA 1988). There is a similar discretion to suspend or adjourn provided in respect of regulated tenancies by s 100 of the RA 1977.

If the court decides to suspend the order on terms and those terms are breached the landlord may apply for a warrant to evict the tenant. The power to suspend or postpone a possession order can be exercised at any time up to the delivery up of possession or execution of the warrant.

8.6.1 Tolerated trespassers and suspended orders for possession

In *Knowlsey Housing Trust v White* [2009] 1 WLR 78, the House of Lords held that an assured tenancy will not end until after the tenant delivers up possession to the landlord, either of his own volition following a possession order or following the execution of the warrant. The Court of Appeal had previously held that an assured tenancy could come to an end if the tenant was in breach of the terms of a suspended possession order (see *Knowsley Housing Trust v White* [2007] 2 WLR 2879). This imported into assured periodic tenancies the concept of the tolerated trespasser which previously had been thought to be confined to public sector tenancies. In order to avoid the numerous difficulties that the creation of 'tolerated trespassers' can cause, the courts would usually grant postponed possession orders rather than suspended possession orders (see para 10.1.2).

Partly in response to the decision of the Court of Appeal, Parliament passed legislation which was designed to abolish the concept of the tolerated trespasser in both assured and public sector tenancies. Part 2 of Sch 11 to the Housing and Regeneration Act 2008 made substantial amendments to the HA 1988 in order to address the problem. These amendments came into force on 19th May 2009.

8.7 Accelerated possession proceedings

Rules 55.11 to 55.19 of the CPR provide an accelerated procedure for obtaining a possession order for premises let on an assured shorthold tenancy without a court hearing. This procedure may be used where the landlord is seeking a possession order only; it cannot be used if the landlord seeks any additional remedy such as a money judgment for rent arrears. The landlord must use Form N5B to commence proceedings. This form is available on the Court Service's website (www.hmcourts-service.gov.uk). The accelerated procedure can only be used in respect of tenancies which were the subject of a written agreement or which followed on from such a tenancy (r 55.12(1) (e) of the CPR). The landlord must include a copy of the tenancy agreement, the s 21 notice and (if applicable) the s 20 notice with the claim form when it is sent to the court for issue.

The court will serve the claim form on the tenant. The documents served will include a blank defence form. If the tenant wishes to oppose the claim or to ask the court to exercise its discretion to postpone the possession under s 89 of the Housing Act 1980 then he must complete this form. The defence form must be served on the landlord and filed at court within 14 days of service of the proceedings. If the defence form is filed the matter will be referred to a judge who will list the matter for a hearing if he is of the view that there may be some merit in the defence.. If the defendant simply seeks extra time (up to 6 weeks) before the possession order becomes effective the matter will only be listed for a hearing if the landlord has not ticked the box in the claim form indicating that he is content for the court to deal with such an application on the papers.

If the tenant does not file a defence form within 14 days the landlord may file a written request for an order for possession. The documents will then be referred to a judge who will make a possession order if he is satisfied that the documents are in order and that the landlord is entitled to possession. If he is not so satisfied then the matter will be listed for a hearing (r 55.16(2) of the CPR).

8.8   Regaining possession

If the tenant remains in possession after the date for possession has passed, the landlord may apply for a warrant for possession under r 17 of Ord 26 of the County Court Rules. The landlord files a request for a warrant using Form N325, available from the Court Service's website (www.hmcourts-service.gov.uk). Upon receipt the court will refer the request to the bailiff who will book an appointment for the execution of the order and notify both parties accordingly. The landlord must apply for a warrant to regain possession if the premises remain occupied after the date for possession has passed (*Hanif v Robinson* [1993] QB 419). If the court made a possession order which was suspended on terms the claimant may apply to the court for a warrant for possession if the tenant breaches the terms of the suspension. If the possession order was made on discretionary grounds the tenant may apply to have the warrant suspended or postponed. If the court does so it will usually impose terms for the payment of rent and arrears if necessary.

8.9   Possession claims online

From 30 October 2006 any claim for possession of residential property based on rent arrears may be commenced using the online procedure provided by the Court Service. Possession Claims Online (PCOL) may not be used if the defendant is a child or protected party as defined by Part 21 of the CPR. The online form serves as both the claim form and the particulars of claim. On receipt of the online form the court will serve a printed copy on the defendant. The defendant may file his defence online but does not have to do so. The court will then issue the proceedings in the appropriate county court which will list the matter for a hearing. Where the proceedings have been commenced using this procedure the parties may also make certain applications online should they wish to do so, such as an application for a warrant for possession.

9 Costs, Public Funding and Court Fees

9.1 Costs

At the conclusion of a case, the general rule is that the unsuccessful party will be ordered to pay the successful party's legal costs. The amount of costs allowed is normally assessed on the standard basis, though if the behaviour of either party has been such as to merit it, or a properly made offer of settlement has been declined, but not beaten at trial, indemnity costs may be awarded. The standard basis allows for costs that are 'proportionate to the matters in issue' with any doubts as to reasonableness or proportionality being resolved in favour of the paying party (r 44.4(2) of the CPR). If the indemnity basis applies, costs will be allowed regardless of proportionality, but those that are unreasonably incurred or unreasonable in amount will be disallowed (r 44.4(1) of the CPR). In practice, a party in whose favour a standard basis costs order is made will usually recover around 75% of his actual costs, and a party with the benefit of an indemnity costs order will usually recover 90% if not all of his actual costs.

9.1.1 Assessment of costs

Since the introduction of the CPR, costs are most frequently summarily assessed at the end of the application or trial. A signed schedule of costs should be filed and served on the other side at least 24 hours before the hearing (PD 43 of the CPR). This should specify:

(a)   the number of hours claimed;

(b)   the hourly rate claimed;

(c)   the grade of fee earner (partner or other experienced solicitor, solicitor of less than 4 years' admission, legal executive or trainee);

(d)   the amount and nature of disbursements claimed;

(e)   solicitor's costs for attending the hearing;

(f)   counsel's fees;

(g)   VAT.

Parties with the benefit of community legal services funding (formally legal aid) are not required to serve such an estimate and summary assessments will not be made of their costs. However, where a costs order is made against a publicly funded party, the amount should be summarily assessed, even if an order is made that the costs order not be enforced without the permission of the court.

At the conclusion of the hearing, the judge will first consider whether to make a costs order at all. Once that is done, a decision will be made as to amount. If the hearing lasts for more than a day, or there has been a multi-track trial, the judge will normally order a detailed assessment. In all other cases the judge will usually conduct a summary assessment of the costs.

9.1.2   Public funding

Frequently, a party to an action arising out of residential premises will be entitled to public funding under the Access to Justice Act 1999. Eligibility for public funding is dependent on satisfying the Legal Services Commission that the nature of the prospective assisted person's case is such as to merit its grant and that he has disposal income and capital that are below certain levels. Only firms which have a contract with the Legal Services Commission may carry out publicly funded work and in practice it can be difficult for an otherwise eligible party to find legal representation. The Legal Services Commission has a charge on any money or other property which is recovered or retained by the assisted person as a result of the proceedings in which he is publicly funded. This charge is up to the extent of the assisted person's actual costs, less any contribution paid by him and any costs recovered from the other side. This charge is subject to certain exemptions.

9.1.3   Recovering costs against a publicly funded opponent

Where an assisted person is the loser, the court can only make an order for costs to be recovered against him after having had regard to all the circumstances, including the means of the parties and their conduct in relation to the case (s 11 of the Access to Justice Act 1999). The usual practice is for the court to make an award on the usual *inter partes* principles and then order that some or all of it not be enforced without permission of the court. The costs protection only applies where the publicly funded party had the benefit of a full public funding certificate. Lesser forms of publicly funded legal assistance such as Legal Help and Help at Court do not afford costs protection.

It should be borne in mind that this restriction on recovering costs applies only where the opponent was actually publicly funded. The fact that he was sufficiently impecunious to be financially eligible for legal aid will not normally affect the operation of the court's discretion on costs. Nor should the assisted person be protected in respect of costs the other party incurred before the assisted person was granted public funding. If the assisted person has taken steps outside the scope of the funding, such as counterclaiming when he had legal aid only to defend, then he will not be protected from a costs order in respect of that (see *Re B (Children)* [2005] EWCA 779).

9.1.4 Recovering costs against the Legal Services Commission

Where the provisions of s 11 of the Access to Justice Act 1999 have prevented a successful party recovering his costs from his opponent, it may be possible to recover them from the legal aid fund itself. The relevant provisions are the Community Legal Services (Costs Protection Regulations) Regulations 2000 (SI 2000/824). The conditions that must be satisfied by the party seeking the award are that:

(a)   the proceedings were commenced by the LSC funded party;

(b)   the party making the application is an individual;

(c)   it is just and equitable for the court to make the award; and

(d)   he would suffer severe financial hardship if the award were not made.

It may be possible for a landlord to recover his costs from the fund where he has successfully resisted a claim by a publicly funded tenant – for instance, for wrongful eviction. Where an order is sought under the Regulations, the normal procedure is for the application to be made at the end of the trial. The judge will, if so inclined, make a provisional award under the section, giving the Legal Services Commission an opportunity to make representations if it wishes before the order becomes final (see para 21.16 of PD 44 of the CPR).

9.2 Fixed costs

In certain circumstances the costs which the successful party may recover from the unsuccessful party may be limited under the CPR. In practice, if the fixed costs regime applies the recoverable costs will be a fraction of the actual costs incurred by a legally represented successful party.

9.2.1 Fixed costs in possession proceedings

Part 45(I) of the CPR sets out the circumstances where a successful claimant will only recover fixed costs from the defendant. In claims for the recovery of land brought under Part 55 the court will only allow the landlord to recover fixed costs if the tenant gives up possession and pays the amount(s) claimed by the landlord before the hearing. In addition, the court will only order the tenant to pay fixed costs where one of the grounds for possession is rent arrears and the tenant has not delivered a defence which does not raise a substantive defence to the landlord's claim for possession. Further, the landlord will only be entitled to fixed costs where he uses the accelerated possession procedure and the tenant does not filed a defence denying his claim. The fixed costs are set out in Table 2 in Part 45. The landlord may additionally recover the issue fee.

In addition to the fixed costs in Table 2, the court may award the cost of obtaining judgment fixed by Part 45.4A. Where the court serves the claim form the allowable costs are currently fixed at £57.25 plus the relevant issue fee and the fixed commencement costs. Where the claimant uses the accelerated possession procedure the solicitors' costs are currently fixed at £79.50, in addition to the issue fee and the fixed commencement costs in Table 2. The fixed costs are altered regularly and reference should be made to the current version of CPR which can be viewed at www.justice.gov.uk.

9.2.2   Fixed costs on the small claims track

If the claim has been allocated to the small claims track the cost are fixed by r 27.14 of the CPR. The successful party can only recover the fixed costs set out in Table 1 to Part 45 (fixed costs on commencement of a claim for the recovery of money or goods), and any court fees he has had to pay. He may recover any travel expenses he or his witness have reasonably incurred in attending court, and any wages he or a witness have lost by attending court, limited to £50 per person (PD 7 of Part 27 of the CPR). The court may only award more than the fixed costs if the paying party has acted unreasonably (r 27.14(2)d)).

9.3   Court fees

Listed below are the amounts of the fees most likely to be incurred in respect of a county court action of the type that is the subject of this book. The court does have a discretion to waive fees in cases of exceptional hardship. The fees are not payable by those in receipt of means tested benefits such as income support. The issue fee and the hearing fee vary according to the track to which the case has been allocated and the size of the claim. Therefore it is important not to overstate any damages which may be recoverable as this will only serve to inflate the fees which the claimant must pay. If the claimant unreasonably overstates the size of his claim then he will probably not recover any overpaid fees from the other side even if he is successful. The fees are payable by the claimant. If a possession claim is dealt with at the initial hearing the only fee payable is the issue fee, save for any fees relating to enforcement.

Issue fee (possession proceedings)	£150
Issue fee (other cases)	£30–£1,530
Issue fee (counterclaim)	£30–£1,530
Issue fee possession proceedings online	£100
Allocation fee	£200
Pre-trial checklist fee	£100
Hearing fee	£25–£1,000
Request for a warrant	£95

10 Related Areas

Like most areas of practice, the law relating private sector residential tenancies can overlap with several other areas. Those which are most likely to be relevant are discussed in the briefest outline below.

10.1 Public sector housing

10.1.1 Secure tenancies

Tenancies granted by local authorities, certain housing associations and other public bodies are generally outside the scope of the Rent Act (RA) 1977 and the parts of the Housing Act (HA) 1988 which have been discussed in this book. They are referred to as secure tenancies and are regulated by the HA 1985. As with assured tenancies the tenancy cannot be brought to an end by the landlord otherwise than obtaining a court order for possession (s 82(1) of the HA 1985). Prior to initiating possession proceedings the landlord must serve a notice seeking possession on the tenant. The notice must be in the prescribed form, it must specify the ground upon which the landlord intends to rely and the particulars of each ground (s 83(2) of the HA 1985). The notice must specify a date after which proceedings may be begun, that date being no earlier than the date upon which the tenancy could have been terminated by notice to quit. As we have seen a notice to quit must give at least 4 weeks' notice and must end on the last day of a period of the tenancy. This provision does not apply where the ground for possession is anti-social behaviour on the part of the tenant or his household. The court has the power to dispense with this notice if it is reasonable to do so.

The grounds upon which the landlord may rely are similar to the grounds available under the HA 1988. Most of the grounds for possession are discretionary grounds, meaning that the court will only make a possession order if it considers it reasonable to do so. The most commonly seen grounds are Ground 1 (failure to pay rent or other breach of covenant), Ground 2 (anti-social behaviour on the part of the tenant or his household) and Ground 2A (domestic violence).

Social landlords must follow the pre-action protocol set out in the Practice Direction to Part 55 of the CPR before bringing possession proceedings based on rent arrears. Other than this the court procedure for obtaining a possession order is the same as that which applies to private sector tenancies.

Section 85 of the HA 1985 gives the court an extended discretionary power to adjourn proceedings, or to stay, postpone or suspend any order which is similar to the power contained in s 9 of the HA 1988. This power can be exercised at any time prior to the execution of the warrant of possession.

10.1.2 Tolerated trespassers

By s 82(2) of the HA 1985 the tenancy will come to an end on the date specified in the possession order upon which the tenant will give up possession. This provision has caused tremendous difficulties for those tenants whose tenancies has been the subject of a suspended possession order. The form of order historically used by the courts meant that in many cases even the most technical breach of the terms of the suspension would operate to terminate the tenancy. This left tenants in an unfortunate 'limbo position' of having a bare right to occupy the premises but no right to enforce any of the landlord's covenants unless they seek a 'revival' of the tenancy under s 85. It has been estimated that up to 20% of public sector tenants in inner London are tolerated trespassers (per Willson LJ in *Jones v Merton LBC* [2008] 4 All ER 287, para 9).

The practical difficulties that this caused both landlords and tenants was removed by Part 1 of Sch 11 to the Housing and Regeneration Act 2008. This amended both the HA 1988 and the HA 1985 with the effect that assured and secure tenancies only come to an end (at the landlord's instigation) when the order for possession is executed. Further, Part 2 of Sch 11 to the Act operates to retrospectively renew any tenancies which have ended pursuant to a possession order where the tenant is still in possession. Schedule 11 came into force on 20th May 2009.

10.2 Homelessness

Part VII of the Housing Act 1996 imposes duties on local housing authorities towards persons who apply for accommodation who are homeless or threatened with homelessness. In brief, local housing authorities are under a duty to secure suitable accommodation for anyone who is homeless or threatened with homelessness, who is in 'priority need' and who has not become homeless intentionally. Applicants will be deemed to be in priority need if they are pregnant or have dependant children, if they are vulnerable due to old age or illness or if they have been made homeless due to an emergency such as flooding or fire. The duty to secure suitable accommodation only applies to persons who have some local connection to the housing authority's area.

In practice, it is difficult to secure housing under this part of the Housing Act in all but the most obvious cases. Housing authorities have to cope with huge demand for limited housing stock. Sometimes, a tenant against whom a possession order is sought is willing to have such an order made against him as he believes that he will then be entitled to council housing because the local authority will not find him to be voluntarily homeless, as it could do if he left without a court order. Such assumptions are not always correct. A tenant who has been evicted due to rent arrears or for breach of covenant is likely to be found to be voluntarily homeless.

If an applicant is dissatisfied with the result of his application he may ask the local authority to conduct a review of the decision. If he is dissatisfied with the review he may bring proceedings in the county court under s 204 of the Housing Act 1996. These proceedings are akin to judicial review and the county court will only quash the decision if it was wrong in law or if it was wholly and demonstrably unreasonable.

10.3   Housing benefit

Many tenants are entitled to receive housing benefit from their local authority in respect of all or part of their rent. The exact entitlement is calculated with regard to the amount of rent the tenant has to pay, the number of dependants he has and his earnings. Tenants who are in receipt of income support and income based jobseekers' allowance are usually entitled to 'full' housing benefit, meaning that they are entitled to the maximum amount payable. With the agreement of the tenant, this benefit may be payable directly to the landlord. The landlord may apply for direct payments if the tenant is more than 8 weeks in arrears. Amongst tenants who are on relatively low incomes and who would be entitled to claim there is a surprisingly high degree of ignorance about this benefit. Those advising such clients should check whether they meet the eligibility criteria.

Applications for housing benefit may take some time to process. The local authority will need proof of income or entitlement to benefits, and proof of the rent payable. Applicants are best advised to bring such documentation to the council in person and obtain receipts from the council for all documents lodged. These documents ought to be brought to any possession hearing where the landlord relies on rent arrears which have been caused by delays in processing the tenant's housing benefit application.

10.4   Business tenancies

These tenancies qualify for a different form of protection which is given by Part II of the Landlord and Tenant Act 1954. Where premises are let for both residential and business purposes, the provisions of the 1954 Act will apply rather than the HA 1988, unless the business use is ancillary to the residential use, for example, *Wright v Mortimer* [1996] EGCS 51, CA. There is no control of the rent payable on the original granting of a business tenancy, although the court may determine the rate for subsequent tenancies. The landlord must renew the tenancy at the end of its term unless certain circumstances apply. If the tenancy is not renewed through no fault of the tenant, he will be entitled to compensation. In practice, it is easy for landlords to opt out of the protection afforded by Landlord and Tenant Act 1954 in respect of new business tenancies.

10.5   Agricultural tenancies

The law relating to tenancies let along with agricultural land or to agricultural employees is exceptionally complex. Some, but not all of these tenancies are capable of being protected or assured tenancies. Even if they are protected tenancies, there are circumstances unique to such tenancies where the landlord may be able to recover possession against the tenant.

10.6   Long leases

A long tenancy is one originally granted for a term of 21 years or more. Such a tenancy will not be a regulated or assured tenancy. There is no prohibition on charging a premium on the assignment of such a tenancy. Indeed, the vast majority of flats which are 'owner occupied' are let on such leases. In some circumstances, the tenant on the expiry of such a lease will be able to extend the lease or acquire the freehold pursuant to the Leasehold Reform Act 1967. These provisions have been supplemented by the Leasehold Reform, Housing and Urban Development Act 1993 which gave further rights of lease renewal for tenants of flats.

11 Common Practical Problems

11.1 Deceased tenant

I have been consulted by a landlord who believes that his tenant has died. The tenancy is now a statutory periodic tenancy by virtue of s 5 of the Housing Act (HA) 1988. As far as he is aware there is no one residing in the premises but he is not sure. He wishes to recover possession. How does he go about it?

Suggested advice

If the tenant was living with his spouse/civil partner at the time of his death then that person is entitled to succeed to the tenancy by virtue of s 17 of the HA 1988. If there was no one entitled to succeed to the tenancy it will have devolved in accordance with the tenant's will or according to the rules of intestacy. If tenant dies intestate and letters of administration have not been taken out in respect of the tenant's estate then the tenancy passes to the public trustee and is no longer assured. In order to bring the periodic tenancy to an end the landlord must service notice on the Public Trustee at the Offices of Court Funds, Official Solicitor and Public Trustee. A copy of the notice must also be sent to the premises addressed to the tenant's personal representatives. Once the tenancy has been terminated the landlord could retake possession of the premises if it is known that there is no one in occupation, however it is always better to err on the side of caution and obtain a possession order. However, the landlord must obtain a possession order if he suspects that the premises may still be occupied. If the landlord is unsure whether the premises are occupied or not he would be best advised to bring possession proceedings. The proceedings ought to be served on the premises addressed to the deceased tenant's personal representatives and on the public trustee.

11.2 Rent increase

I have been consulted by a tenant whose landlord says he wants to raise the rent on his flat. Is the landlord entitled to do this?

Suggested advice

Firstly, check the terms of the written tenancy agreement (if any). If the tenancy does not provide for a rent increase and it is an assured periodic tenancy the landlord must first serve a notice that he intends increasing the rent pursuant to s 13 of the Housing Act 1988. The tenant is then entitled to refer the notice to a rent assessment committee who can decide by how much, if anything, the rent should be increased. The landlord cannot unilaterally increase the rent during the fixed term of the tenancy unless there is a term within the tenancy agreement which permits him to do so. However, such a term may be held to be unfair within the meaning of the Unfair Terms in Consumer Contracts Regulations 1999 (SI 1999/2083) and could therefore be unenforceable (see para 6.4.1).

If it was granted before 15 January 1989 next establish whether there is a fair rent registered in respect of the flat. The tenant may know the answer himself. If he does not know, the Rent Service will be able assist. If there is a registered rent, the landlord can only raise the rent to that which has been registered. If 2 years have passed since the last registration, he is entitled to apply for it to be reassessed. If there is no registered rent and the tenancy has always been a periodic one, the landlord can charge what he likes, subject to any contractual restraint. If the tenancy has become a statutory one, the landlord must first serve a notice of increase as prescribed in s 45 of the Rent Act 1977. In any case, if the tenant feels that he is being overcharged, he should make an application for a fair rent to be assessed.

11.3   Sitting tenant

My client has recently inherited a house that is the subject of a long standing Rent Act tenancy. Although he believes the present tenants are satisfactory, he would like to be able to obtain possession, as he wishes to live there himself. Can he do this?

Proposed advice

The court can make a possession order under Case 9 of Sch 15 to the Rent Act 1977 on the grounds that the landlord wishes to live there himself unless the landlord acquired his interest by purchase, which someone who inherits a property, of course, does not do. The court will, however, order possession only if it considers it reasonable to do so. Where there are long-standing tenants, and the landlord has his own accommodation, it is unlikely that the court would make such an order. The court might be more inclined to do so if the landlord were in a position to offer the tenants suitable alternative accommodation, in which case s 98(1)(a) of the 1977 Act might assist.

11.4   Noisy tenant

I was consulted by a landlord who is anxious to regain possession of premises recently let to a tenant who persistently holds noisy parties. He wrote a letter to the tenant a month ago telling him he must leave. Can he start proceedings yet?

Suggested advice

Normally, a court will only order possession if a valid notice pursuant to s 8 of the Housing Act 1988 has been served. It does not sound as if this letter constituted a proper notice. Such a notice must contain prescribed information (see Appendix A, para 9). Once the notice has been served, as the possession claim will be based on Ground 14 proceedings can be served immediately. If proceedings had been commenced without the service of a notice, the court will have a discretion to waive this requirement. However, if the tenancy is shorthold and the fixed term has either ended or has little time to run, the landlord may obtain possession of the premises more quickly if serves notice under s 21 of the HA 1988 and commences accelerated possession proceedings.

11.5   Harassed tenant

My client lives in a single room bedsit and has fallen behind with his rent. His landlord says he is only has a licence of the room has repeatedly threatened to throw him out of the bedsit and changed the locks. My client is very worried he may carry out his threat. What should he do?

Suggested advice

Firstly, the landlord cannot evict the client without a court order, even if he is a licencee not a tenant. A classic lawyer's response to this scenario will be to apply for emergency public funding and go to court for an injunction preventing the landlord from taking any steps to evict or threaten the client. However, advisors may also wish to consider enlisting the assistance of the local authority. Many have dedicated officers charged with dealing with cases of actual or threatened illegal eviction and it is worth bearing in mind that it is the local authority which is the prosecuting authority in cases of unlawful eviction. If the client is concerned about his safety then an immediate application should be made for an emergency injunction.

11.6   Students

I have been consulted by some students from the local university. Three months ago they were granted what their landlord described as a 'student tenancy'. The landlord has now decided that he wants to evict them. He has not given any reason for this. He has told them that as they are students, they do not have any rights as tenants. Is this correct?

Suggested advice

It seems likely that your clients are in fact assured shorthold tenants. Students are, of course, entitled to the same rights as anyone else. The only exception is where the tenancy has been granted by a specified educational institution or body of persons (para 8 of Sch 1 to the HA 1988). This provision applies only if the tenants are students, but regardless of whether they are studying at the institution which granted the tenancy. If para 8 does apply, then the landlord will be entitled to possession once the contractual term of the tenancy has expired, though the landlord will still have to obtain a court order.

11.7   Resident landlord

My clients have been given a notice to quit by their landlord. He has told them that they are not tenants and only have a 'licence'. The reason he gives for this is that he lives in the top floor flat of the same house, which has four storeys. My clients live in the basement. Is what the landlord says correct, and if it is, do my clients have any protection from being evicted?

Suggested advice

The tenancy is subject to the 'resident landlord' exception contained in Sch 1 to the Housing Act 1988. The question of whether they are tenants or licencees is fairly academic. If there is a tenancy, it will not be given any statutory protection by reason of para 10 of Sch 1 to the Housing Act 1988. This provides that where landlord and tenant live in the same building, even in different self-contained flats (unless it is a purpose built block), the landlord will be able to obtain possession so long as the contractual term and/or a valid notice to quit have expired. A thorough history of the landlord's occupation must be taken from the tenant. If the landlord moved in after the commencement of the tenancy or if he ceased residing in the building as his only or principal home at any time during the tenancy then the tenancy will no longer be exempted from protection.

Tenants in this situation are protected by the Protection from Eviction Act 1977. The landlord must terminate the tenancy and commence possession proceedings in order to regain possession. Tenants and licencees who share their actual accommodation with the landlord and/or a member of the landlord's family do not have even this protection (s 3A of the Protection from Eviction Act 1977).

11.8   Old shorthold tenancy

In 1996, my client entered into a written tenancy agreement with his tenant. The tenancy is described on the face of the agreement as being an assured shorthold tenancy. The tenancy agreement has been renewed every year. My client is unable to locate his copy of the s 20 notice. The client wishes to recover possession and the tenant has indicated he does not want to leave. How should we proceed?

Suggested advice

The initial tenancy commenced prior to the entry into force of the Housing Act 1996 and in the premises it will not be shorthold unless the landlord served a valid s 20 notice on the tenant before the tenancy agreement was entered into. It is for the landlord to prove that the tenancy is shorthold. It will be difficult for him to do this without a copy of the notice. If he is sure that he did, in fact, serve the notice they the court may willing to accept this evidence. Further, if the tenant still has a copy of the notice then he will have to disclose it in the course of the proceedings. However, it is more likely than not that the court will not be satisfied that the notice was served and the landlord may wish to consider settling the matter with his tenant, for example by offering to compensate him for moving out.

11.9   Unauthorised occupier

My client has let a flat under a periodic assured shorthold tenancy. It has come to his attention that the tenant has allowed a third party to reside in the premises without telling him. The client believes that the tenant has left, and is now in rent arrears. My client wants to regain possession. What can he do?

Suggested advice

The client ought to commence possession proceedings against his tenant. If the tenant is no longer in occupation the tenancy is no longer assured and can be terminated by notice to quit. This will operate to terminate any sub-tenancy granted by the tenant. However, the client is best advised to also serve a notice under s 21 of the HA

1988 without prejudice to the validity of the notice to quit. He may rely on this in the alternative to his claim for possession based on the notice to quit.

If the third party is still in occupation after the date upon which the possession order takes effect, the bailiff may still enforce any warrant against that person notwithstanding the fact that he was not a party to the proceedings. Note that the client must inform the court of the fact that there is a third party in occupation when he completes Form N119 (particulars of claim for possession)

However, the client should be aware of the fact that the third party may seek to be joined to and defend the proceedings on the basis that he has some right to remain in the premises that has not been lawfully terminated, or that the head tenancy has not been lawfully terminated.

12   Procedural Checklists

12.1 Representing the landlord at a possession hearing (assured tenancy)

1.   Have the claim form and particular of claim been duly served?

2.   Have both the claim form and the particulars of claim been duly signed with a statement of truth by an appropriate person?

3.   Do the particulars of claim comply with PD 2.1 of Part 55 of the CPR?

4.   Has the landlord attached a copy of the written tenancy agreement (if any) to the particulars of claim?

5.   Has the tenancy agreement been stamped (only relevant if granted prior to 1 December 2003 and the annual rent exceeds £5,000)?

6.   Has the relevant notice been served and is there evidence of service?

7.   If the landlord has served the claim form is there evidence of service?

8.   Has the landlord served a witness statement? If not will there be anyone present at the hearing to give evidence on behalf of the landlord?

9.   Has the tenant served a defence form? Are any facts admitted (and so need not be proved)?

10.   If necessary, ensure that the court is aware of the case of *North British Housing Association v Matthews* [2005] 1 WLR 3133 and the limits it places on the courts jurisdiction to adjourn in cases were a mandatory ground is made out.

11.   If an order is granted has the court specified the grounds upon which the order is made?

12.2 Representing the landlord at in a possession action based on rent arrears

1.   As steps 1–11 in para 12.1.

2.   Has the landlord complied with PD 4 of Part 55 of the CPR?

3.   Is the schedule of arrears up to date?

4.   What were the arrears at the date of service of the s 8 notice?

5.   Have any steps been taken to discuss the rent arrears with the tenant?

6.   If the landlord is a registered social landlord, has it complied with the pre-action protocol for possession actions based on rent arrears?

12.3 Representing the landlord in a possession claim based on s 21 of the HA 1988

1.   As steps 1–10 in para 12.1.

2.   Is there a written tenancy agreement? If not the matter cannot be dealt with under the accelerated possession procedure.

3.   Have copies of the s 21 notice (and s 20 notice if relevant) and the tenancy agreement been attached to the particulars of claim?

4.   Has the court already declined to deal with the matter under the accelerated possession procedure? If so why?

5.   Does the s 21 notice expire on the correct day?

6.   Does the tenant contest service/validity of the s 21 notice?

7.   Has the landlord complied with the provisions of the HA 2006 relating to deposits?

12.4 Representing the tenant in a claim based on rent arrears

1.   Has the landlord complied with steps 1–8 in para 12.1?

2.   Does the client have an outstanding claim for housing benefit?

3.   Can the client appeal any adverse decision regarding housing benefit?

4.   Does the client have written proof of his application for housing benefit and/or any proof of documents supplied to the local authority in respect of his income and the rent payable?

5.   What is the client's income? What payments can he afford to make towards the rent arrears?

6.   Will the landlord agree to an adjournment on terms?

7.   Does the client have any potential counterclaim against his landlord for example for disrepair?

12.5 Representing the tenant in a possession claim based on s 21 of the HA 1988

1. Has the landlord duly complied with steps 1–7 in para 12.1 and steps 2–7 in para 12.3?

2. Does the tenant recall receiving the s 21 notice. If not does landlord have proof of service of the s 21 notice?

3. Does it expire on the correct day?

4. Does the tenant want to ask for extra time (up to 6 weeks) to move out? What are his grounds and has he included this in the defence form?

Appendix A
Suggested Forms and Precedents

1   Agreement for a residential tenancy

This agreement is made on [15th March 2009] between: [AB] (hereinafter called the landlord) for one part and [CD] (hereinafter called the tenant) for the other part AND IT IS AGREED as follows:

1.   The landlord lets to the tenants the premises known as [9, Eden Park, Auckland, County Durham] together with the fixtures, fittings, furniture and effects therein (hereinafter called the contents) which are specified in the attached inventory signed by the landlord and the tenants for a term of [12 months] (hereinafter called the term) commencing on the [1st April 2009] at a rent of [£750] per [month] to be paid in advance on the [1st] day of each [month] except that the first such payment shall be due on the date hereof.

1.   The tenant agrees to:

(i)   pay the rent on the days and in the manner as aforesaid;

(ii)   pay for all gas and electricity consumed or supplied on or to the premises (including all fixed and standing charges) and to pay all council tax which falls due in respect of the premises, and all charges for the maintenance and use of the 'land line' telephone on the premises during the term;

(iii)   keep the interior of the premises clean and tidy and in as good and tenantable state of repair and decorative condition as at the beginning of the term, reasonable wear and tear and damage by fire excepted;

(iv)   not damage or injure the premises;

(v)   use the premises in and only in a tenant-like manner;

(vi)   keep the contents clean, in good repair and condition and where applicable in working order, reasonable wear and tear and damage by fire being excepted;

(vii)   replace any of the contents which may be destroyed or damaged so as to be unusable other than through fair wear and tear or by fire with others of similar value and appearance;

[(viii) keep the garden clean and tidy and in a proper state of cultivation;]

(ix) not remove any of the contents from the premises;

(x) not carry on any trade, business or profession upon the premises nor receive paying guests but use the premises only as a private residence for a maximum of [two] residents;

(xi) not exhibit any poster or notice so as to be visible from the exterior of the premises;

(xii) not permit or allow to be done on the premises anything which may be or become a nuisance or annoyance to the landlord or the occupiers of any adjoining premises or which may render the landlord's insurance of the premises void or voidable or increase the rate of premium for such insurance;

(xiii) not use or allow the premises to be used for any illegal or immoral purpose;

(xiv) not make any noise or play any radio, television set, record player, CD player, musical instrument or other similar device at the premises between 11 pm and 8 am so as to be audible outside the premises;

(xv) not block or cause any blockage to the drains and pipe gutters and channels in or about the premises;

(xvi) not assign, underlet or part with possession of the whole or any part of the premises;

(xvii) permit the landlord and the landlord's agents at reasonable times in daylight by appointment to enter the premises during the last 28 days of the term with prospective tenants and during any part of the term with prospective purchasers of the landlord's interest in the premises;

(xviii) permit the landlord and the landlords agents to enter the premises for the purposes of carrying out repairs or other works thereto, the landlord undertaking to give the tenant one week's written notice of his intention to carry out such works save where such works are urgently required.

(xix) notify the landlord forthwith in writing of any defects in the premises as soon as practicable after such defects come to the notice of the tenant; and

(xx) at the end of the term:

  (a) yield up the premises and the contents in such state of repair and condition as shall be in accordance with the tenant's obligations under this agreement;

(b) make good or pay for the repair or replacement of such of the contents as have been broken, lost or damaged during the term other than through fair wear and tear or by fire;

(c) pay for the washing (including ironing and pressing) of all linen and for the washing and cleaning (including ironing and pressing) of all blankets and curtains and similar items which have been soiled during the tenancy; and

(d) leave the contents in the rooms and places in which they were at the commencement of the term.

2.   The landlord agrees to:

(i)   permit the tenant, so long as they pay the rent and perform their obligations under this agreement, quietly to use and enjoy the premises during the term without any interruption from the landlord or any person rightfully claiming under or in trust for the landlord;

(ii)   return to the tenant any rent payable for any period during which the premises may have been rendered uninhabitable by fire or any other risk against which the landlord has insured.

If

(i)   any part of the rent is in arrears for more than 14 days whether formally demanded or not; or

(ii) if there is any breach of any of the tenants' obligations under this agreement; or

(iii) if the premises are without the agreement of the landlord left unoccupied for a continuous period in excess of 4 weeks,

the landlord may re-enter the premises and thereupon the tenancy created by this agreement will determine, but without prejudice to any other rights and remedies of the landlord.

3.   The Deposit

No deposit is payable in respect of this tenancy agreement OR

The landlord acknowledges the receipt from the tenants of the sum of £750 by way of deposit. The landlord intends to [place the deposit in an accredited tenancy deposit scheme OR retain the deposit and enter into an accredited insurance scheme], details of the scheme which the landlord has chosen and further information on the law relating to tenancy deposits will be supplied to the tenant within 14 days hereof. The tenants will not be entitled to repayment of the deposit or any part thereof until possession shall be yielded up to the landlord.

4.   Services of Notices

Any notice which the landlord may seek to serve on the tenant will be deemed to be validly served if left at the premises addressed to the tenant or if sent in ordinary first class post addressed the tenant at the premises.

Signed by the landlord

Landlord's signature witnessed by [name and address]

[Signature of witness] Signed by tenant

Tenant's signature witnessed by [name and address]

[Signature of witness]

Note: this example is for use where the tenancy is for a fixed term, with rent payable monthly, and is furnished. It can be adapted quite simply where the terms are different. It will normally have the effect of creating an assured shorthold tenancy.

2   Agreement for a residential tenancy which is not an assured shorthold tenancy due to the licensor residing in the same building

This agreement is made on [15th March 2008] between: [EF] (hereinafter called 'the licensor') for one part, and [GH] (hereinafter called 'the licencee') for the other part.

IT IS AGREED as follows:

That the licensor will allow the licencee to occupy the basement flat in the premises known as and situate at [100 Grace Road, Leicester] (the said flat hereinafter being referred to as 'the premises') and have the use of the fixtures, fittings, furniture and effects therein which are specified in the attached inventory signed by the licensor and the licencee and collectively referred to herein as 'the contents' for a term of [six months] (hereinafter called the term) commencing on [1st April 2008] in consideration for the payment by the licencee of a fee of [£500] per month to be paid in advance on the 1st day of each month save that the first such payment is to be made on the date hereof.

1.   The licencee agrees to:

(i)   pay the fee on the days and in the manner aforesaid;

(ii)   pay for all gas and electricity consumed or supplied on or to the premises (including all fixed and standing charges) and all charges for the maintenance and use of the telephone on the premises during the term;

(iii)   keep the interior of the premises clean and tidy and in as good a state of repair and decorative order as at the beginning of the term, fair wear and tear and damage by fire excepted;

(iv)   not damage or injure the premises;

(v)   use the premises only in a responsible manner, having regard to the proximity of the licensor in the other parts of the said 100 Grace Road, and in particular will not:

   (a) at any time play a radio, record or CD player, television, musical instrument or similar apparatus so that it can be heard in the other parts of the said 100 Grace Road or so that it causes nuisance or annoyance to anyone not on the premises;

   (b) at any time have more than eight people, including the licencee, in the premises; and

   (c) between the hours of midnight and 8 am have more than two people, including the licencee, in the premises;

(vi)   keep the contents clean, in good repair and where applicable working order; reasonable wear and tear, mechanical breakdown not caused by misuse, and fire damage being excepted;

(vii)   replace any of the contents which may be destroyed or damaged in breach of clause (vii) above;

(viii)   not remove any of the contents from the premises or from the respective positions in the premises which they occupy at the commencement of the term;

(ix)   not carry on any trade, business or profession upon the premises nor receive paying guests but use the premises only as a private residence for the licencee only;

(x)   not exhibit any poster or notice so as to be visible from the exterior of the premises;

(xi)   not use the premises for any illegal or immoral purpose;

(xii)   permit the licensor to enter the premises at any hour for any purpose;

(xiii)   at the end of the term yield up the premises and contents in such state of repair and condition as shall be in accordance with the licencees' obligations under this agreement.

2.   The licensor agrees to:

(i)   pay and indemnify the licencee against all council tax assessments and outgoings and all water and sewerage charges in respect of the premises.

3   Services of Notices

Any notice which the licensor may seek to serve on the licencee will be deemed to be validly served if left at the premises addressed to the licencee or if sent in ordinary first class post addressed the licencee at the premises.

This agreement is personal to the licencee and may not be assigned by [him] and will terminate automatically if the licencee ceases to reside at the premises.

If any part of the fee is not paid and becomes more than 14 days in arrears (whether or not formally demanded) or if the licencee breaches any of [his] obligations under this agreement the licencee will be deemed to have forfeited his right to occupy the premises and the licensor may treat the premises as no longer occupied by the licencee whereupon all rights the licencee has under this agreement will terminate, without prejudice to any of the licensor's other rights under this agreement.

Signed by the licensor

Licensor's signature witnessed by [name and address] [Signature of witness]

Signed by licencee

Licencee's signature witnessed by [name and address] [Signature of witness]

Note: even if the above agreement in fact is a tenancy and not a licence, it cannot be an assured tenancy by virtue of para 10 to Sch 1 to the HA 1988.

3   Endorsement on a tenancy agreement which is to be subject to Grounds 1 and 2 of Sch 2 to the HA 1988, where landlord has previously lived in the property

To the tenant [IJ]: TAKE NOTICE that the landlord, [KL], has at some time before the beginning of this tenancy occupied the dwelling house which is the subject of this tenancy as his only or principal residence and may recover possession thereof under the provisions of Ground 1 of Schedule 2 to the Housing Act 1988. AND FURTHER TAKE NOTICE that the dwelling house which is the subject of the tenancy is subject to a mortgage granted to the [Whichever] Building Society/Bank and that under the said mortgage the said Building Society/Bank may in certain circumstances be entitled to exercise a power of sale conferred on it by the mortgage and/or section 101 of the Law of Property Act 1925 and the said Building Society may recover possession thereof in pursuance of that power under the provisions of Ground 2 of the Housing Act 1988.

Signed [Landlord or agent]

I/we acknowledge receipt of a notice of which this is a true copy
Signed [tenant]

4 Endorsement on a tenancy agreement which is to be subject to Grounds 1 and 2 of Sch 2 to the HA 1988, where landlord has not previously lived in the property

To the tenant [JI]: TAKE NOTICE that the landlord [KL] may in due course require the dwelling as his or his spouse's only or principal home and that in such event may recover possession thereof under the provisions of Ground 3 of Schedule 2 to the Housing Act 1988.

AND FURTHER TAKE NOTICE [continue as in 3 above] ...

5 Notice that tenancy is not to be an assured shorthold tenancy, served on tenant before tenancy commences

Take notice:

To: [CD],

The tenancy of 9 Eden Park, Auckland, Co Durham which is to be granted to you commencing on 1 December 2009 is not to be an assured shorthold tenancy.

Signed [AB]

6 Notice of landlord's address

Section 48 of the Landlord and Tenant Act 1987

To the tenant: [CD of 9 Eden Park, Auckland Co Durham]

Please note that the address at which notices concerning the above property, including notices in proceedings, may be served on your landlord [AB] is [landlord's address]

Signed [landlord or agent]

7 Notice to quit addressed to a tenant

NOTICE TO QUIT (SERVED BY LANDLORD'S AGENT) To [MN] of [68 Sabina Park, Kingston, Surrey]:

We [name of agent giving notice] on behalf of your landlord(s) [OP] of 1, The Hill, Sydenham, London], give you notice to quit and deliver up possession to him of [68 Sabina Park, Kingston, Surrey] on 24 January 2009 or the day on which a complete period of your tenancy expires next after the end of 4 weeks from the service of this notice.

Date [1 December 2008] Signed [Solicitor or other agent]

The name and address of the agent who served this notice is [name and address].

Information for tenant

1. If the tenant or licencee does not leave the dwelling, the landlord or licensor must get an order for possession from the court before the tenant or licencee can lawfully be evicted. The landlord or licensor cannot apply for such an order before the notice to quit or notice to determine has run out.

2. A tenant or licencee who does not know if he has any right to remain in possession after a notice to determine runs out can obtain advice from a solicitor. Help with all or part of the cost of legal advice and assistance may be available under the Legal Aid Scheme. He should also be able to obtain information from a Citizens' Advice Bureau, a Housing Aid Centre or a rent officer.

Notes:

1 Notice to quit any premises let as a dwelling must be given at least four weeks before it takes effect and it must be in writing (s 5 of the Protection from Eviction Act 1977).

2 Where a notice to quit is given by a landlord to determine a tenancy of any premises let as a dwelling, the notice must contain this information (Notice to Quit etc (Prescribed Information) Regulations 1988 (SI 1988/2201)).

8 Notice seeking possession served during the fixed term; s 21(1) of the HA 1988

To: CD the tenant of 9 Eden Park Auckland Co Durham,

I, AB, of 92 Trent Bridge, Nottingham, Bristol, hereby give you notice that I require possession by virtue of the Housing Act 1988, s 21(1), of the said 9 Eden Park on or after 20th April 2010 or after the expiry of two months from the date of service of this notice whichever date is the sooner.

Dated 15ᵗʰ February 2010

9 Notice seeking possession served after the expiry of the fixed term; s 21(4) of the HA 1988

To: CD the tenant of 9 Eden Park Auckland Co Durham,

I, AB, of 92 Trent Bridge, Nottingham, Bristol, hereby give you notice that I require possession by virtue of the Housing Act 1988 s 21(4), of 9 Eden Park, Auckland, Co Durham after 31ˢᵗ June 2010, or after the last day of the period of your tenancy which ends after the expiry of two months from the date of service of this notice, whichever date is the sooner.

Dated 15ᵗʰ April 2010

10 Notice seeking possession; s 8(4) of the HA 1988

Housing Act 1988 section 8 as amended by section 151 of the Housing Act 1996

Notice seeking possession of a property let on an Assured Tenancy or an Assured Agricultural Occupancy

– Please write clearly in black ink

– Please tick boxes where appropriate and cross out text marked with an asterisk (*) that does not apply.

– This form should be used where possession of accommodation let under an assured tenancy, an assured agricultural occupancy or an assured shorthold tenancy is sought on one of the grounds in Schedule 2 to the Housing Act 1988.

– Do not use this form if possession is sought on the 'shorthold' ground under section 21 of the Housing Act 1988 from an assured shorthold tenant where the fixed term has come to an end or, for assured shorthold tenancies with no fixed term which started on or after 28th February 1997, after six months has elapsed. There is no prescribed form for these cases, but you must give notice in writing.

1. To:

Name(s) of tenant(s)/licencee(s)*

2. Your landlord/licensor* intends to apply to the court for an order
requiring you to give up possession of:

Address of premises

3. Your landlord/licensor* intends to seek possession on ground(s)

in Schedule 2 to the Housing Act 1988, as amended by the Housing
Act 1996, which read(s):

_Give the full text (as set out in the Housing Act 1988 as amended by the Housing
Act 1996) of each ground which is being relied on. Continue on a separate sheet
if necessary._

4. Give a full explanation of why each ground is being relied on:

Continue on a separate sheet if necessary.

Notes on the grounds for possession

* If the court is satisfied that any of grounds 1 to 8 is established,
  it must make an order (but see below in respect of fixed term
  tenancies).

- Before the court will grant an order on any of grounds 9 to 17, it must be satisfied that it is reasonable to require you to leave. This means that, if one of these grounds is set out in section 3, you will be able to suggest to the court that it is not reasonable that you should have to leave, even if you accept that the ground applies.

- The court will not make an order under grounds 1, 3 to 7, 9 or 16, to take effect during the fixed term of the tenancy (if there is one) and it will only make an order during the fixed term on grounds 2, 8, 10 to 15 or 17 if the terms of the tenancy make provision for it to be brought to an end on any of these grounds.

- Where the court makes an order for possession solely on ground 6 or 9, the landlord must pay your reasonable removal expenses.

5. The court proceedings will not begin until after:

_____

Give the earliest date on which court proceedings can be brought

Where the landlord is seeking possession on grounds 1, 2, 5 to 7, 9 or 16, court proceedings cannot begin earlier than 2 months from the date this notice is served on you (even where one of grounds 3, 4, 8, 10 to 13, 14A, 15 or 17 is specified) and not before the date on which the tenancy (had it not been assured) could have been brought to an end by a notice to quit served at the same time as this notice.

Where the landlord is seeking possession on grounds 3, 4, 8, 10 to 13, 14A, 15 or 17, court proceedings cannot begin earlier than 2 weeks from the date this notice is served (unless one of 1, 2, 5 to 7, 9 or 16 grounds is also specified in which case they cannot begin earlier than two months from the date this notice is served)

Where the landlord is seeking possession on ground 14 (with or without other grounds), court proceedings cannot begin before the date this notice is served.

Where the landlord is seeking possession on ground 14A, court proceedings cannot begin unless the landlord has served, or has taken all reasonable steps to serve, a copy of this notice on the partner who has left the property.

After the date shown in section 5, court proceedings may be begun at once but not later than 12 months from the date on which this notice is served. After this time the notice will lapse and a new notice must be served before possession can be sought.

6. Name and address of landlord/licensor.*

To be signed and dated by the landlord or licensor or his agent (someone acting for him). If there are joint landlords each landlord or the agent must sign unless one signs on behalf of the rest with their agreement.

Signed	Date

Please specify whether: landlord licensor ☐ joint landlords ☐ landlord's agent ☐

Name(s) (Block Capitals)

_____

_____

Address

_____

_____

_____

Telephone – Daytime

_____

Evening

_____

What to do if this notice is served on you

This notice is the first step requiring you to give up possession of your home. You should read it very carefully.

Your landlord cannot make you leave your home without an order for possession issued by a court. By issuing this notice your landlord is informing you that he intends to seek such an order. If you are willing to give up possession without a court order, you should tell the person who signed this notice as soon as possible and say when you are prepared to leave. Whichever grounds are set out in section 3 of this form, the court may allow any of the other grounds to be added at a later date. If this is done, you will be told about it so you can discuss the additional grounds at the court hearing as well as the grounds set out in section 3.

If you need advice about this notice, and what you should do about it, take it immediately to a citizens' advice bureau, a housing advice centre, a law centre or a solicitor.

11 Witness statement in support of possession claim (rent arrears)

In the County Court Case No

In the Matter of *[address of premises]*

Between AB Claimant

and

CD Defendant

Statement of AB

1.   I make this statement in support of my application for possession of the premises at [9 Eden Park Auckland Co Durham (hereinafter called 'the premises').

2.   I am the freehold owner of the premises having purchased them on 19 March 2000 from the previous owners Mr and Mrs Artemus Jones.

3.   On 15ᵗʰ March 2009 I entered into a tenancy agreement with CD in respect of the above premises. The term of the tenancy was 12 months and the monthly rent of £750 was to be paid on the 1ˢᵗ of every month. A copy of the tenancy agreement is attached hereto and marked Exhibit AB1.

4.   The tenants have failed to pay the rent due. On 2 September 2009 I served a notice on the tenants pursuant to s 8 of the Housing Act 1988 relying on grounds 8, 10 and 11 of Schedule II to the Act. The notice was served by me by posting it through the letterbox of the property. As at the date of service of the notice the rent arrears amounted to [£1,500]. A copy of that notice is attached hereto and marked Exhibit AB II.

5.   As at the date of this witness statement the arrears stand at [£2,250] I have attached to the Particulars of Claim a full schedule of the amounts which have fallen due under the ten-

ancy agreement and the amounts which the tenants have paid. I believe that the tenants continue to reside in the property. I have attempted to contact the tenants by telephone to discuss the arrears without success. I respectfully ask the court to grant a possession order in respect of the premises and judgment in respect of the arrears owning as at the date of the hearing.

I believe/the Claimant believes the facts stated in this statement are true

Signed_____ Date_____

12   Particulars of claim for disrepair

In the County Court Case No

In the Matter of *[address of premises]*

Between   CD   Claimant

and

AB   Defendant

Particulars of claim

1.   The Defendant is the freehold owner of the premises known as and situate at 9 Eden Park, Auckland, Co Durham ('the premises').

2.   By a written agreement made on 15th March 2009 the Defendant granted an assured shorthold tenancy to the Claimant for a term of 12 months at a rent of £750 per month.

3.   It was an express term of the agreement that the claimant would [particularise any relevant covenant to repair contained within the tenancy agreement]

4.   Further by virtue of s 11 of the Landlord and Tenant Act 1985 there was implied into the tenancy agreement a term that the Defendant would;

(i) keep in repair the structure and exterior of the property including the drains gutters and external pipes, and

(ii) keep in repair and proper working order the installations for in the dwelling house for the supply of gas water an electricity and for sanitation, and

(iii) keep in repair and proper working order the installations for space and water heating.

5.   In breach of the above covenants the Defendant has permitted the premises to fall into a state of disrepair.

PARTICULARS

[Particularise the defects present in the premises]

1. The Claimant notified the defendant of the defects set out in paragraph 5 above on 2nd April 2009. To date the Defendant has not remedied the said defects.

2. By reason of the Defendant's breach of covenant the Claimant's use and enjoyment of the premises has been compromised. Further the claimants have sustained loss and damage. A schedule of loss is attached hereto

6.   The Claimant claims and is entitled to interest at the rate of 2% in respect of general damages and 6% in respect of special damage for such period as the court deems fit pursuant to s 69 of the County Courts Act 1984.

And the Claimant claims:

(i)   An injunction requiring the Defendant to remedy the defects set out herein

(ii)   Damages

(iii)   Interest as aforesaid

I believe the facts stated in these particulars of claim are true

Signed _____ Date_____

        CD

Appendix B
Part 55 of the CPR

[Reproduced under the terms of the Click-Use Licence]

55.1 Interpretation

In this Part –

(a) 'a possession claim' means a claim for the recovery of possession of land (including buildings or parts of buildings);

(b) 'a possession claim against trespassers' means a claim for the recovery of land which the claimant alleges is occupied only by a person or persons who entered or remained on the land without the consent of a person entitled to possession of that land but does not include a claim against a tenant or sub-tenant whether his tenancy has been terminated or not;

(c) 'mortgage' includes a legal or equitable mortgage and a legal or equitable charge and 'mortgagee' is to be interpreted accordingly;

(d) 'the 1985 Act' means the Housing Act 1985;

(e) 'the 1988 Act' means the Housing Act 1988;

(f) 'a demotion claim' means a claim made by a landlord for an order under section 82A of the 1985 Act or section 6A of the 1988 Act ('a demotion order');

(g) 'a demoted tenancy' means a tenancy created by virtue of a demotion order; and

(h) 'a suspension claim' means a claim made by a landlord for an order under section 121A of the 1985 Act.

I GENERAL RULES

55.2 Scope

(1) The procedure set out in this Section of this Part must be used where the claim includes –

(a) a possession claim brought by a –

(i) landlord (or former landlord);

(ii) mortgagee; or

(iii) licensor (or former licensor);

(b) a possession claim against trespassers; or

(c)   a claim by a tenant seeking relief from forfeiture.

(Where a demotion claim or a suspension claim (or both) is made in the same claim form in which a possession claim is started, this Section of this Part applies as modified by rule 65.12. Where the claim is a demotion claim or a suspension claim only, or a suspension claim made in addition to a demotion claim, Section III of Part 65 applies).

(2)   This Section of this Part

(a)   is subject to any enactment or practice direction which sets out special provisions with regard to any particular category of claim;

(b)   does not apply where the claimant uses the procedure set out in Section II of this Part; and

(c)   does not apply where the claimant seeks an interim possession order under Section III of this Part except where the court orders otherwise or that Section so provides.

55.3 Starting the claim

(1)   The claim must be started in the county court for the district in which the land is situated unless paragraph (2) applies or an enactment provides otherwise.

(2)   The claim may be started in the High Court if the claimant files with his claim form a certificate stating the reasons for bringing the claim in that court verified by a statement of truth in accordance with rule 22.1(1).

(3)   The practice direction refers to circumstances which may justify starting the claim in the High Court.

(4)   Where, in a possession claim against trespassers, the claimant does not know the name of a person in occupation or possession of the land, the claim must be brought against 'persons unknown' in addition to any named defendants.

(5)   The claim form and form of defence sent with it must be in the forms set out in the relevant practice direction.

55.4 Particulars of claim

The particulars of claim must be filed and served with the claim form.

(The relevant practice direction and Part 16 provide details about the contents of the particulars of claim)

55.5 Hearing date

(1)   The court will fix a date for the hearing when it issues the claim form.

(2)   In a possession claim against trespassers the defendant must be served with the claim form, particulars of claim and any witness statements –

(a) in the case of residential property, not less than 5 days; and

(b) in the case of other land, not less than 2 days,

before the hearing date.

(3)   In all other possession claims –

(a) the hearing date will be not less than 28 days from the date of issue of the claim form;

(b) the standard period between the issue of the claim form and the hearing will be not more than 8 weeks; and

(c) the defendant must be served with the claim form and particulars of claim not less than 21 days before the hearing date.

(Rule 3.1(2)(a) provides that the court may extend or shorten the time for compliance with any rule)

55.6 Service of claims against trespassers

Where, in a possession claim against trespassers, the claim has been issued against 'persons unknown', the claim form, particulars of claim and any witness statements must be served on those persons by –

(a)

(i) attaching copies of the claim form, particulars of claim and any witness statements to the main door or some other part of the land so that they are clearly visible; and

(ii) if practicable, inserting copies of those documents in a sealed transparent envelope addressed to 'the occupiers' through the letter box; or

(b)   placing stakes in the land in places where they are clearly visible and attaching to each stake copies of the claim form, particulars of claim and any witness statements in a sealed transparent envelope addressed to 'the occupiers'.

55.7 Defendant's response

(1)   An acknowledgment of service is not required and Part 10 does not apply.

(2)   In a possession claim against trespassers rule 15.2 does not apply and the defendant need not file a defence.

(3)   Where, in any other possession claim, the defendant does not file a defence within the time specified in rule 15.4, he may take

part in any hearing but the court may take his failure to do so into account when deciding what order to make about costs.

(4)   Part 12 (default judgment) does not apply in a claim to which this Part applies.

55.8 The hearing

(1)   At the hearing fixed in accordance with rule 55.5(1) or at any adjournment of that hearing, the court may –

(a) decide the claim; or

(b) give case management directions.

(2)   Where the claim is genuinely disputed on grounds which appear to be substantial, case management directions given under paragraph (1)(b) will include the allocation of the claim to a track or directions to enable it to be allocated.

(3)   Except where –

(a) the claim is allocated to the fast track or the multi-track; or

(b) the court orders otherwise,

any fact that needs to be proved by the evidence of witnesses at a hearing referred to in paragraph (1) may be proved by evidence in writing.

(Rule 32.2(1) sets out the general rule about evidence. Rule 32.2(2) provides that rule 32.2(1) is subject to any provision to the contrary)

(4)   Subject to paragraph (5), all witness statements must be filed and served at least 2 days before the hearing.

(5)   In a possession claim against trespassers all witness statements on which the claimant intends to rely must be filed and served with the claim form.

(6)   Where the claimant serves the claim form and particulars of claim, must produce at the hearing a certificate of service of those documents and rule does not apply.

55.9 Allocation

(1)   When the court decides the track for a possession claim, the matters to which it shall have regard include –

(a) the matters set out in rule 26.8 as modified by the relevant practice direction;

(b) the amount of any arrears of rent or mortgage instalments;

(c) the importance to the defendant of retaining possession of the land;

(d) the importance of vacant possession to the claimant; and

(e) if applicable, the alleged conduct of the defendant

(2)   The court will only allocate possession claims to the small claims track if all the parties agree.

(3)   Where a possession claim has been allocated to the small claims track the claim shall be treated, for the purposes of costs, as if it were proceeding on the fast track except that trial costs shall be in the discretion of the court and shall not exceed the amount that would be recoverable under rule 46.2 (amount of fast track costs) if the value of the claim were up to £3,000.

(4)   Where all the parties agree the court may, when it allocates the claim, order that rule 27.14 (costs on the small claims track) applies and, where it does so, paragraph (3) does not apply.

55.10 Possession claims relating to mortgaged residential property

(1)   This rule applies where a mortgagee seeks possession of land which consists of or includes residential property.

(2)   Not less than 14 days before the hearing the claimant must send a notice to the property addressed to 'the occupiers'.

(3)   The notice referred to in paragraph (2) must –

(a) state that a possession claim for the property has started;

(b) show the name and address of the claimant, the defendant and the court which issued the claim form; and

(c) give details of the hearing.

(4)   The claimant must produce at the hearing –

(a) a copy of the notice; and

(b) evidence that he has served it.

55.10A Electronic issue of certain possession claims

(1)   A practice direction may make provision for a claimant to start certain types of possession claim in certain courts by requesting the issue of a claim form electronically.

(2)   The practice direction may, in particular –

(a) provide that only particular provisions apply in specific courts;

(b) specify –

(i) the type of possession claim which may be issued electronically;

(ii) the conditions that a claim must meet before it may be issued electronically;

(c) specify the court where the claim may be issued;

(d) enable the parties to make certain applications or take further steps in relation to the claim electronically;

(e) specify the requirements that must be fulfilled in relation to such applications or steps;

(f) enable the parties to correspond electronically with the court about the claim;

(g) specify the requirements that must be fulfilled in relation to electronic correspondence;

(h) provide how any fee payable on the filing of any document is to be paid where the document is filed electronically.

(3)   The Practice Direction may disapply or modify these Rules as appropriate in relation to possession claims started electronically.

II ACCELERATED POSSESSION CLAIMS OF PROPERTY LET ON AN ASSURED SHORTHOLD TENANCY

55.11 When this section may be used

(1)   The claimant may bring a possession claim under this Section of this Part where –

(a) the claim is brought under section 21 of the 1988 Act[2] to recover possession of residential property let under an assured shorthold tenancy; and

(b) subject to rule 55.12(2), all the conditions listed in rule 55.12(1) are satisfied.

(2)   The claim must be started in the county court for the district in which the property is situated.

(3)   In this Section of this Part, a 'demoted assured shorthold tenancy' means a demoted tenancy where the landlord is a registered social landlord.

(By virtue of section 20B of the 1988 Act, a demoted assured shorthold tenancy is an assured shorthold tenancy.)

55.12 Conditions

(1)   The conditions referred to in rule 55.11(1)(b) are that –

(a) the tenancy and any agreement for the tenancy were entered into on or after 15 January 1989;

(b) the only purpose of the claim is to recover possession of the property and no other claim is made;

(c) the tenancy did not immediately follow an assured tenancy which was not an assured shorthold tenancy;

(d) the tenancy fulfilled the conditions provided by section 19A or 20(1)(a) to (c) of the 1988 Act

(e) the tenancy

(i) was the subject of a written agreement;

(ii) arises by virtue of section 5 of the 1988 Act but follows a tenancy that was the subject of a written agreement; or

(iii) relates to the same or substantially the same property let to the same tenant and on the same terms (though not necessarily as to rent or duration) as a tenancy which was the subject of a written agreement; and

(f) a notice in accordance with sections 21(1) or 21(4) of the 1988 Act was given to the tenant in writing.

(2)   If the tenancy is a demoted assured shorthold tenancy, only the conditions in paragraph (1)(b) and (f) need be satisfied.

55.13 Claim form

(1)   The claim form must –

(a) be in the form set out in the relevant practice direction; and

(b)

(i) contain such information; and

(ii) be accompanied by such documents,

as are required by that form.

(2)   All relevant sections of the form must be completed.

(3)   The court will serve the claim form by first class post (or an alternative service which provides for delivery on the next working day).

55.14 Defence

(1)   A defendant who wishes to –

(a) oppose the claim; or

(b) seek a postponement of possession in accordance with rule 55.18,

must file his defence within 14 days after service of the claim form.

(2)   The defence should be in the form set out in the relevant practice direction.

55.15 Claim referred to judge

(1)   On receipt of the defence the court will –

(a) send a copy to the claimant; and

(b) refer the claim and defence to a judge.

(2)　Where the period set out in rule 55.14 has expired without the defendant filing a defence –

(a) the claimant may file a written request for an order for possession; and

(b) the court will refer that request to a judge.

(3)　Where the defence is received after the period set out in rule 55.14 has expired but before a request is filed in accordance with paragraph (2), paragraph (1) will still apply.

(4)　Where –

(a) the period set out in rule 55.14 has expired without the defendant filing a defence; and

(b) the claimant has not made a request for an order for possession under paragraph (2) within 3 months after the expiry of the period set out in rule 55.14,

the claim will be stayed.

55.16 Consideration of the claim

(1)　After considering the claim and any defence, the judge will –

(a) make an order for possession under rule 55.17;

(b) where he is not satisfied as to any of the matters set out in paragraph (2) –

(i) direct that a date be fixed for a hearing; and

(ii) give any appropriate case management directions, or

(c) strike out the claim if the claim form discloses no reasonable grounds for bringing the claim.

(2)　The matters referred to in paragraph (1)(b) are that –

(a) the claim form was served; and

(b) the claimant has established that he is entitled to recover possession under section 21 of the 1988 Act against the defendant.

(3)　The court will give all parties not less than 14 days' notice of a hearing fixed under paragraph (1)(b)(i).

(4)　Where a claim is struck out under paragraph (1)(c) –

(a) the **55.17 Possession order**

Except where rules 55.16(1)(b) or (c) apply, the judge will make an order for possession without requiring the attendance of the parties.

55.18 Postponement of possession

(1)   Where the defendant seeks postponement of possession on the ground of exceptional hardship under section 89 of the Housing Act 1980, the judge may direct a hearing of that issue.

(2)   Where the judge directs a hearing under paragraph (1) –

(a) the hearing must be held before the date on which possession is to be given up; and

(b) the judge will direct how many days' notice the parties must be given of that hearing.

(3)   Where the judge is satisfied, on a hearing directed under paragraph (1), that exceptional hardship would be caused by requiring possession to be given up by the date in the order of possession, he may vary the date on which possession must be given up.

55.19 Application to set aside or vary

55.19

The court may

(a)   on application by a party within 14 days of service of the order; or

(b)   of its own initiative,

set aside or vary any order made under rule 55.17.

III INTERIM POSSESSION ORDERS

(omitted)

PRACTICE DIRECTION – POSSESSION CLAIMS

1.1

Except where the county court does not have jurisdiction, possession claims should normally be brought in the county court. Only exceptional circumstances justify starting a claim in the High Court.

1.2

If a claimant starts a claim in the High Court and the court decides that it should have been started in the county court, the court will normally either strike the claim out or transfer it to the county court on its own initiative. This is likely to result in delay and the court will normally disallow the costs of starting the claim in the High Court and of any transfer.

1.3

Circumstances which may, in an appropriate case, justify starting a claim in the High Court are if –

(1)   there are complicated disputes of fact;

(2)   there are points of law of general importance; or

(3)   the claim is against trespassers and there is a substantial risk of public disturbance or of serious harm to persons or property which properly require immediate determination.

1.4

The value of the property and the amount of any financial claim may be relevant circumstances, but these factors alone will not normally justify starting the claim in the High Court.

1.5

The claimant must use the appropriate claim form and particulars of claim form set out in Table 1 to Part 4 Practice Direction. The defence must be in form N11, N11B, N11M or N11R, as appropriate.

1.6

High Court claims for the possession of land subject to a mortgage will be assigned to the Chancery Division.

1.7

A claim which is not a possession claim may be brought under the procedure set out in Section I of Part 55 if it is started in the same claim form as a possession claim which, by virtue of rule 55.2(1) must be brought in accordance with that Section.

(Rule 7.3 provides that a claimant may use a single claim form to start all claims which can be conveniently disposed of in the same proceedings)

1.8

For example a claim under paragraphs 4, 5 or 6 of Part I of Schedule 1 to the Mobile Homes Act 1983 may be brought using the procedure set out in Section I of Part 55 if the claim is started in the same claim form as a claim enforcing the rights referred to in section 3(1)(b) of the Caravan Sites Act 1968 (which, by virtue of rule 55.2(1) must be brought under Section I of Part 55).

1.9

Where the claim form includes a demotion claim, the claim must be started in the county court for the district in which the land is situated.

55.4 – PARTICULARS OF CLAIM

2.1

In a possession claim the particulars of claim must:

(1)   identify the land to which the claim relates;

(2)   state whether the claim relates to residential property;

(3)   state the ground on which possession is claimed;

(4)   give full details about any mortgage or tenancy agreement; and

(5)   give details of every person who, to the best of the claimant's knowledge, is in possession of the property.

Residential property let on a tenancy

2.2

Paragraphs 2.3 to 2.4B apply if the claim relates to residential property let on a tenancy.

2.3

If the claim includes a claim for non-payment of rent the particulars of claim must set out:

(1)   the amount due at the start of the proceedings;

(2)   in schedule form, the dates and amounts of all payments due and payments made under the tenancy agreement for a period of two years immediately preceding the date of issue, or if the first date of default occurred less than two years before the date of issue from the first date of default and a running total of the arrears;

(3)   the daily rate of any rent and interest;

(4)   any previous steps taken to recover the arrears of rent with full details of any court proceedings; and

(5)   any relevant information about the defendant's circumstances, in particular:

    (a) whether the defendant is in receipt of social security benefits; and

    (b) whether any payments are made on his behalf directly to the claimant under the Social Security Contributions and Benefits Act 1992.

2.3A

If the claimant wishes to rely on a history of arrears which is longer than two years, he should state this in his particulars and exhibit a full (or longer) schedule to a witness statement.

2.4

If the claimant knows of any person (including a mortgagee) entitled to claim relief against forfeiture as underlessee under section 146(4) of the Law of Property Act 1925 (or in accordance with section 38 of the Supreme Court Act 1981, or section 138(9C) of the County Courts Act 1984):

(1)   the particulars of claim must state the name and address of that person; and

(2)   the claimant must file a copy of the particulars of claim for service on him.

2.4A

If the claim for possession relates to the conduct of the tenant, the particulars of claim must state details of the conduct alleged.

2.4B

If the possession claim relies on a statutory ground or grounds for possession, the particulars of claim must specify the ground or grounds relied on.

Land subject to a mortgage

2.5 (OMITTED)

Possession claim against trespassers

2.6

If the claim is a possession claim against trespassers, the particulars of claim must state the claimant's interest in the land or the basis of his right to claim possession and the circumstances in which it has been occupied without licence or consent.

Possession claim in relation to a demoted tenancy by a housing action trust or a local housing authority

2.7

If the claim is a possession claim under section 143D of the Housing Act 1996 (possession claim in relation to a demoted tenancy where the landlord is a housing action trust or a local housing authority), the particulars of claim must have attached to them a copy of the notice to the tenant served under section 143E of the 1996 Act.

55.5 – HEARING DATE

3.1

The court may exercise its powers under rules 3.1(2)(a) and (b) to shorten the time periods set out in rules 55.5(2) and (3).

3.2

Particular consideration should be given to the exercise of this power if:

(1)   the defendant, or a person for whom the defendant is responsible, has assaulted or threatened to assault:

(a) the claimant;

(b) a member of the claimant's staff; or

(c) another resident in the locality;

(2)   there are reasonable grounds for fearing such an assault; or

(3)   the defendant, or a person for whom the defendant is responsible, has caused serious damage or threatened to cause serious damage to the property or to the home or property of another resident in the locality.

3.3

Where paragraph 3.2 applies but the case cannot be determined at the first hearing fixed under rule 55.5, the court will consider what steps are needed to finally determine the case as quickly as reasonably practicable.

55.6 – SERVICE IN CLAIMS AGAINST TRESPASSERS

4.1

If the claim form is to be served by the court and in accordance with rule 55.6(b) the claimant must provide sufficient stakes and transparent envelopes.

55.8 – THE HEARING

5.1

Attention is drawn to rule 55.8(3). Each party should wherever possible include all the evidence he wishes to present in his statement of case, verified by a statement of truth.

5.2

If relevant the claimant's evidence should include the amount of any rent or mortgage arrears and interest on those arrears. These amounts should, if possible, be up to date to the date of the hearing (if necessary by specifying a daily rate of arrears and interest). However, rule 55.8(4) does not prevent such evidence being brought up to date orally or in writing on the day of the hearing if necessary.

5.3

If relevant the defendant should give evidence of:

(1)   the amount of any outstanding social security or housing benefit payments relevant to rent or mortgage arrears; and

(2)   the status of:

    (a) any claims for social security or housing benefit about which a decision has not yet been made; and

    (b) any applications to appeal or review a social security or housing benefit decision where that appeal or review has not yet concluded.

5.4

If:

(1)   the maker of a witness statement does not attend a hearing; and

(2)   the other party disputes material evidence contained in his statement,

the court will normally adjourn the hearing so that oral evidence can be given.

CONSUMER CREDIT ACT CLAIMS RELATING TO THE RECOVERY OF LAND

7.1

Any application by the defendant for a time order under section 129 of the Consumer Credit Act 1974 may be made:

(1)   in his defence; or

(2)   by application notice in the proceedings.

ENFORCEMENT OF CHARGING ORDER BY SALE

7.2

A party seeking to enforce a charging order by sale should follow the procedure set out in rule 73.10 and the Part 55 procedure should not be used.

SECTION II – ACCELERATED POSSESSION CLAIMS OF PROPERTY LET ON AN ASSURED SHORTHOLD TENANCY

55.18 – POSTPONEMENT OF POSSESSION

8.1

If the judge is satisfied as to the matters set out in rule 55.16(2), he will make an order for possession in accordance with rule 55.17, whether or not the defendant seeks a postponement of possession on the ground of exceptional hardship under section 89 of the Housing Act 1980.

8.2

In a claim in which the judge is satisfied that the defendant has shown exceptional hardship, he will only postpone possession without directing a hearing under rule 55.18(1) if –

(1)   he considers that possession should be given up 6 weeks after the date of the order or, if the defendant has requested postponement to an earlier date, on that date; and

(2)   the claimant indicated on his claim form that he would be content for the court to make such an order without a hearing.

8.3

In all other cases if the defendant seeks a postponement of possession under section 89 of the Housing Act 1980, the judge will direct a hearing under rule 55.18(1).

8.4

If, at that hearing, the judge is satisfied that exceptional hardship would be caused by requiring possession to be given up by the date in the order of possession, he may vary that order under rule 55.18(3) so that possession is to be given up at a later date. That later date may be no later than 6 weeks after the making of the order for possession on the papers (see section 89 of the Housing Act 1980).

Practice Direction – Possession Claims Online

[Reproduced under the terms of the Click-Use Licence]

This Practice Direction supplements CPR rule 55.10A.

Scope of this practice direction

1.1

This practice direction provides for a scheme ('Possession Claims Online') to operate in specified county courts –

(1) enabling claimants and their representatives to start certain possession claims under CPR Part 55 by requesting the issue of a claim form electronically via the PCOL website; and

(2) where a claim has been started electronically, enabling the claimant or defendant and their representatives to take further steps in the claim electronically as specified below.

1.2

In this practice direction –

(1) 'PCOL website' means the website www.possessionclaim.gov. uk which may be accessed via Her Majesty's Courts Service website (www.hmcourts-service.gov.uk) and through which Possession Claims Online will operate; and

(2) 'specified court' means a county court specified on the PCOL website as one in which Possession Claims Online is available.

Information on the PCOL website

2.1

The PCOL website contains further details and guidance about the operation of Possession Claims Online.

2.2

In particular the PCOL website sets out –

(1) the specified courts; and

(2) the dates from which Possession Claims Online will be available in each specified court.

2.3

The operation of Possession Claims Online in any specified court may be restricted to taking certain of the steps specified in this practice direction, and in such cases the PCOL website will set out the steps which may be taken using Possession Claims Online in that specified court.

Security

3.1

Her Majesty's Courts Service will take such measures as it thinks fit to ensure the security of steps taken or information stored electronically. These may include requiring users of Possession Claims Online –

(1) to enter a customer identification number or password;

(2) to provide personal information for identification purposes; and

(3) to comply with any other security measures,

before taking any step online.

Fees

4.1

A step may only be taken using Possession Claims Online on payment of the prescribed fee where a fee is payable. Where this practice direction provides for a fee to be paid electronically, it may be paid by –

(1) credit card;

(2) debit card; or

(3) any other method which Her Majesty's Courts Service may permit.

4.2

A defendant who wishes to claim exemption from payment of fees must do so through an organisation approved by Her Majesty's Courts Service before taking any step using PCOL which attracts a fee. If satisfied that the defendant is entitled to fee exemption, the organisation will submit the fee exemption form through the PCOL website to Her Majesty's Courts Service. The defendant may then use PCOL to take such a step.

(Her Majesty's Courts Service website contains guidance as to when the entitlement to claim an exemption from payment of fees arises. The PCOL website will contain a list of organisations through which the defendant may claim an exemption from fees).

Claims which may be started using Possession Claims Online

5.1

A claim may be started online if –

(1) it is brought under Section I of Part 55;

(2) it includes a possession claim for residential property by –

(a) a landlord against a tenant, solely on the ground of arrears of rent (but not a claim for forfeiture of a lease); or

(b) a mortgagee against a mortgagor, solely on the ground of default in the payment of sums due under a mortgage,

relating to land within the district of a specified court;

(3) it does not include a claim for any other remedy except for payment of arrears of rent or money due under a mortgage, interest and costs;

(4) the defendant has an address for service in England and Wales; and

(5) the claimant is able to provide a postcode for the property.

5.2

A claim must not be started online if a defendant is known to be a child or protected party.

Starting a claim

6.1

A claimant may request the issue of a claim form by –

(1) completing an online claim form at the PCOL website;

(2) paying the appropriate issue fee electronically at the PCOL website or by some other means approved by Her Majesty's Courts Service.

6.2

The particulars of claim must be included in the online claim form and may not be filed separately. It is not necessary to file a copy of the tenancy agreement, mortgage deed or mortgage agreement with the particulars of claim.

6.2A

In the case of a possession claim for residential property that relies on a statutory ground or grounds for possession, the claimant must specify, in section 4(a) of the online claim form, the ground or grounds relied on.

6.3

Subject to paragraphs 6.3A and 6.3B, the particulars of claim must include a history of the rent or mortgage account, in schedule form setting out –

(1) the dates and amounts of all payments due and payments made under the tenancy agreement, mortgage deed or mortgage agreement either from the first date of default if that date occurred less than two years before the date of issue or for a period of two years immediately preceding the date of issue; and

(2) a running total of the arrears.

6.3A

Paragraph 6.3B applies where the claimant has, before commencing proceedings, provided the defendant in schedule form with –

(1) details of the dates and amounts of all payments due and payments made under the tenancy agreement, mortgage deed or mortgage account –

(a) for a period of two years immediately preceding the date of commencing proceedings; or

(b) if the first date of default occurred less than two years before that date, from the first date of default; and

(2) a running total of the arrears.

6.3B

Where this paragraph applies the claimant may, in place of the information required by paragraph 6.3, include in his particulars of claim a summary only of the arrears containing at least the following information –

(1) The amount of arrears as stated in the notice of seeking possession served under either section 83 of the Housing Act 1985 or section 8 of the Housing Act 1988, or at the date of the claimant's letter before action, as appropriate;

(2) the dates and amounts of the last three payments in cleared funds made by the defendant or, if less than three payments have been made, the dates and amounts of all payments made;

(3) the arrears at the date of issue, assuming that no further payments are made by the defendant.

6.3C

Where the particulars of claim include a summary only of the arrears the claimant must –

(1) serve on the defendant not more than 7 days after the date of issue, a full, up-to-date arrears history containing at least the information required by paragraph 6.3; and

(2) either – ·

(a) make a witness statement confirming that he has complied with sub-paragraph (1) or (2) of paragraph 6.3A as appropriate, and including or exhibiting the full arrears history; or

(b) verify by way of oral evidence at the hearing that he has complied with sub-paragraph (1) or (2) of paragraph 6.3A as appropriate and also produce and verify the full arrears history.

(Rule 55.8(4) requires all witness statements to be filed and served at least 2 days before the hearing.)

6.4

If the claimant wishes to rely on a history of arrears which is longer than two years, he should state this in his particulars and exhibit a full (or longer) schedule to a witness statement.

6.5

When an online claim form is received, an acknowledgment of receipt will automatically be sent to the claimant. The acknowledgment does not constitute notice that the claim form has been issued or served.

6.6

When the court issues a claim form following the submission of an online claim form, the claim is 'brought' for the purposes of the Limitation Act 1980 and any other enactment on the date on which the online claim form is received by the court's computer system. The court will keep a record, by electronic or other means, of when online claim forms are received.

6.7

When the court issues a claim form it will –

(1) serve a printed version of the claim form and a defence form on the defendant; and

(2) send the claimant notice of issue by post or, where the claimant has supplied an e-mail address, by electronic means.

6.8

The claim shall be deemed to be served on the fifth day after the claim was issued irrespective of whether that day is a business day or not.

6.9

Where the period of time within which a defence must be filed ends on a day when the court is closed, the defendant may file his defence on the next day that the court is open.

6.10

The claim form shall have printed on it a unique customer identification number or a password by which the defendant may access the claim on the PCOL website.

6.11

PCOL will issue the proceedings in the appropriate county court by reference to the post code provided by the claimant and that court shall have jurisdiction to hear and determine the claim and to carry out enforcement of any judgment irrespective of whether the property is within or outside the jurisdiction of that court.

(CPR 30.2(1) authorises proceedings to be transferred from one county court to another.)

Defence

7.1

A defendant wishing to file –

(1) a defence; or

(2) a counterclaim (to be filed together with a defence) to a claim which has been issued through the PCOL system, may, instead of filing a written form, do so by –

> (a) completing the relevant online form at the PCOL website; and

> (b) if the defendant is making a counterclaim, paying the appropriate fee electronically at the PCOL website or by some other means approved by Her Majesty's Courts Service.

7.2

Where a defendant files a defence by completing the relevant online form, he must not send the court a hard copy.

7.3

When an online defence form is received, an acknowledgment of receipt will automatically be sent to the defendant. The acknowledgment does not constitute notice that the defence has been served.

7.4

The online defence form will be treated as being filed –

(1) on the day the court receives it, if it receives it before 4 p.m. on a working day; and

(2) otherwise, on the next working day after the court receives the online defence form.

7.5

A defence is filed when the online defence form is received by the court's computer system. The court will keep a record, by electronic or other means, of when online defence forms are received.

Statement of truth

8.1

CPR Part 22 requires any statement of case to be verified by a statement of truth. This applies to any online claims and defences and application notices.

8.2

CPR Part 22 also requires that if an applicant wishes to rely on matters set out in his application notice as evidence, the application notice must be verified by a statement of truth. This applies to any application notice completed online that contains matters on which the applicant wishes to rely as evidence.

8.3

Attention is drawn to –

(1) paragraph 2 of the practice direction supplementing CPR Part 22, which stipulates the form of the statement of truth; and

(2) paragraph 3 of the practice direction supplementing CPR Part 22, which provides who may sign a statement of truth; and

(3) CPR 32.14, which sets out the consequences of making, or causing to be made, a false statement in a document verified by a statement of truth, without an honest belief in its truth.

Signature

9.1

Any provision of the CPR which requires a document to be signed by any person is satisfied by that person entering his name on an online form.

Communication with the court electronically by the messaging service

10.1

If the PCOL website specifies that a court accepts electronic communications relating to claims brought using Possession Claims Online the parties may communicate with the court using the messaging service facility, available on the PCOL website ('the messaging service').

10.2

The messaging service is for brief and straightforward communications only. The PCOL website contains a list of examples of when it will not be appropriate to use the messaging service.

10.3

Parties must not send to the court forms or attachments via the messaging service.

10.4

The court shall treat any forms or attachments sent via the messaging service as not having been filed or received.

10.5

The court will normally reply via the messaging service where –

(1) the response is to a message transmitted via the messaging service; and

(2) the sender has provided an e-mail address.

Electronic applications

11.1

Certain applications in relation to a possession claim started online may be made electronically ('online applications'). An online application may be made if a form for that application is published on the PCOL website ('online application form') and the application is made at least five clear days before the hearing.

11.2

If a claim for possession has been started online and a party wishes to make an online application, he may do so by –

(1) completing the appropriate online application form at the PCOL website; and

(2) paying the appropriate fee electronically at the PCOL website or by some other means approved by Her Majesty's Courts Service.

11.3

When an online application form is received, an acknowledgment of receipt will automatically be sent to the applicant. The acknowledgment does not constitute a notice that the online application form has been issued or served.

11.4

Where an application must be made within a specified time, it is so made if the online application form is received by the court's computer system within that time. The court will keep a record, by electronic or other means, of when online application forms are received.

11.5

When the court receives an online application form it shall –

(1) serve a copy of the online application endorsed with the date of the hearing by post on the claimant at least two clear days before the hearing; and

(2) send the defendant notice of service and confirmation of the date of the hearing by post; provided that

(3) where either party has provided the court with an e-mail address for service, service of the application and/or the notice of service and confirmation of the hearing date may be effected by electronic means.

Request for issue of warrant

12.1

Where –

(1) the court has made an order for possession in a claim started online; and

(2) the claimant is entitled to the issue of a warrant of possession without requiring the permission of the court

the claimant may request the issue of a warrant by completing an online request form at the PCOL website and paying the appropriate fee electronically at the PCOL website or by some other means approved by Her Majesty's Courts Service.

12.2

A request under paragraph 12.1 will be treated as being filed –

(1) on the day the court receives the request, if it receives it before 4 p.m. on a working day; and

(2) otherwise, on the next working day after the court receives the request.

(CCR Order 26 rule 5 sets out certain circumstances in which a warrant of execution may not be issued without the permission of the court. CCR Order 26 rule 17(6) applies rule 5 of that Order with necessary modifications to a warrant of possession.)

Application to suspend warrant of possession

13.1

Where the court has issued a warrant of possession, the defendant may apply electronically for the suspension of the warrant, provided that:

(1) the application is made at least five clear days before the appointment for possession; and

(2) the defendant is not prevented from making such an application without the permission of the court.

13.2

The defendant may apply electronically for the suspension of the warrant, by –

(1) completing an online application for suspension at the PCOL website; and

(2) paying the appropriate fee electronically at the PCOL website or by some other means approved by Her Majesty's Courts Service.

13.3

When an online application for suspension is received, an acknowledgment of receipt will automatically be sent to the defendant. The acknowledgment does not constitute a notice that the online application for suspension has been served.

13.4

Where an application must be made within a specified time, it is so made if the online application for suspension is received by the court's computer system within that time. The court will keep a record, by electronic or other means, of when online applications for suspension are received.

13.5

When the court receives an online application for suspension it shall –

(1) serve a copy of the online application for suspension endorsed with the date of the hearing by post on the claimant at least two clear days before the hearing; and

(2) send the defendant notice of service and confirmation of the date of the hearing by post; provided that

(3) where either party has provided the court with an e-mail address for service, service of the application and/or the notice of service and confirmation of the hearing date may be effected by electronic means.

Viewing the case record

14.1

A facility will be provided on the PCOL website for parties or their representatives to view –

(1) an electronic record of the status of claims started online, which will be reviewed and, if necessary, updated at least once each day; and

(2) all information relating to the case that has been filed by the parties electronically.

14.2

In addition, where the PCOL website specifies that the court has the facility to provide viewing of such information by electronic means, the parties or their representatives may view the following information electronically –

(1) court orders made in relation to the case; and

(2) details of progress on enforcement and subsequent orders made.